seattle 3rd edition

eat.shop seattle was researched,
photographed and written by kaie wellman

eat

shop

17

about eat.shop

the first thing to know about the *eat.shop guides* is that they are the only guides dedicated to just eating and shopping. okay, we list some hotels, because we know that you need to sleep. and don't forget to whittle out some time for cultural activities—all of the businesses featured in the book are helmed by creative types who are highly influenced by the arts and sights of the cities they live in—culture is good for you.

the *eat.shop guides* feature approximately 90 carefully picked businesses, all of them homegrown and distinctive. some are small and some are big. some are posh and some are street-style. some are spendy and some require nothing more than pocket change. some are old school and some are shiny and new. some are hip and some are under-the-radar. point being, we like to feature a mix of places that are unique because you can feel the passionate vision of the owners from the moment you step through their door, eat their food, touch their wares.

enough explaining, here are a couple of things to remember when using this guide: remember that hours change seasonally, so always call or check the website before you go. we apologize if a featured business has closed. being a small business can be a rough road and some of our featured ones don't make it—so use this book often and support the little guys! remember that items mentioned may not be available any longer, but there will most likely be something equally fantastic available. finally, each guide has a two-year life span, and each new edition is different than the last—so when the 4th edition of eat.shop seattle comes out in 2009, make sure to keep this first edition as it will still be useful.

if you don't own the past editions, you'll love the new feature on the page after next. here you'll find a complete listing of all of the businesses that have been featured in the past two editions. these businesses are listed by neighborhood, and you can all their pertinent information on the eat.shop website. and by the end of 2007, these businesses original spreads will be available online to view. remember—every business that has been featured in this book, past and presence, is fantastic. if the business is no longer featured in the book, it's not because i no longer love the business, but because there are so many incredible businesses that are deserving to be noted. so make sure to reference this list also, as many of seattle's true gems are on it and are not to be missed.

kaie's notes on seattle

in the two years since the last edition of eat.shop seattle came out, many things have changed in the emerald city. first and foremost, the restaurant scene has exploded. when i was doing my research for this edition, i found that the list for the eat side of the book was incredibly long. it was not easy to make the final choices, but let me tell you, it was pure pleasure doing the research. you'll find a mix of not only brand spankin' new places, but also some beloved seattle institutions. the shopping scene also evolved quite a bit, with some really fresh new places debuting. and west seattle gets special mention, as the shopping opportunities over the bridge make it well worth the drive over, even if you live in on the other side of town.

eat, shop and enjoy.

kaie wellman (kaie@eatshopguides.com)

the master list

columbia city / beacon hill / georgetown

eat:

columbia city bakery
el quetzal
galaxie espresso
geraldine's counter

shop:

george

west seattle

eat:

bakery nouveau
beato food & wine
husky deli

shop:

clementine
click! design that fits
divina
georgia blu
moxie papergoods & gifts
swee swee paperie & studio

pioneer square / international district

eat:

green leaf
maneki

shop:

a mano
betty lin
kobo
maison luxe
ornamo
riveted
tulip
watson kennedy

belltown / pike place market / downtown / south lake union / queen anne

eat:

nielsen's pastries
steelhead diner
tavolata
vessel

shop:

david smith & co
fancy pants
la rousse
oslo's
peter miller
polite society
rue
schmancy
tune
tuuli
urchin
watson kennedy
(2nd location)

eastlake / first hill / capitol hill / madrona / madison valley

eat:

café stellina
coco la ti da
cremant
dinette
frites
george's sausage & delicatessen
havana cocktail club
joe bar
la spiga osteria
lark
licorous
remedy teas
sitka & spruce
saint-germain
victrola coffee roaster
volunteer park café & marketplace

shop:

fleurish
hitchcock
juniper
lavender heart
red ticking
tricoter
two owls
veritables

fremont / phinney ridge / green lake / wallingford / ballard

eat:

copper gate
fresh flours
mighty-o donuts
oliver's twist
olsen's scandinavian foods
paseo caribbean
35th street bistro
trophy cupcakes and party
volterra

shop:

bitters co.
blackbird
clover
essenza
flit
frock shop
impulse
kimberly bakery jewelry
lambs ear
les amis
merge
mimi rose
okok
private screening
space oddity
tableau
velouria

previous edition businesses

columbia city / beacon hill / georgetown

eat:
all city coffee (gt)
la medusa (cc)
tutta bella neapolitan pizzeria (cc)

west seattle

eat:
cupcake royale
mission
mashiko
west 5

shop:
retroactive kids
sweetie

pioneer square / international district

eat:
big john's pfi (id)
collins pub (ps)
grand central bakery (ps)
panama hotel tea & coffee house (id)
tamarind tree (id)
zeitgeist coffee (ps)

shop:
flux inc.

belltown / pike place market / downtown / south lake union / queen anne

eat:
alibi room (ppm)
brasa (bt)
café campagne (ppm)
campagne (ppm)
el diablo coffee co. (qa)
le pichet (bt)
macrina bakery and café (bt)
marjorie (bt)
mistral (bt)
resturant zöe (bt)
shorty's (bt)
top pot doughnuts (bt)
union (ppm)
viceroy (bt)
zig zag café (ppm)

shop:
adelita (qa)
encanto barcelona (ppm)
fini (ppm)
great jones home (bt)
isadora (bt)
kuhlman (bt)
flora and henri (dt)
french quarter (bt)
paperhaus (bt)
pike & western wine shop (ppm)
sway & cake (dt)
tbc (dt)
3 x 10 (bt)
velocity art and design (bt)
world spice merchants (ppm)

eastlake / u district / maple leaf / first hill / capitol hill / madrona / madison valley / madison park

eat:
agua verde café (ud)
baguette box (ch)
bandoleone (el)
chapel (ch)
crave (ch)
crush (mv)
cupcake royale (m)
harvest vine (mv)
judy fu's snappy dragon (ml)
kingfish café (ch)
linda's tavern (ch)
machiavelli (ch)
monsoon (ch)
pair (ud)
serafina (el)
st. clouds restaurant (m)
tango (ch)
the hi – spot café (m)
vios café & marketplace (ch)
voila bistro (mv)

shop:
area 51 (ch)
canopy blue (mv)
décor on 34th (m)
fetch (m)
frenchy's (mv)
goods (ch)
martha e. harris flowers & gifts (mp)
pearson & gray (mp)
plum (mv)
square room (ch)
wall of sound (ch)

fremont / phinney ridge / green lake / wallingford / ballard

eat:
blue c sushi (fre)
cupcake royale (bal)
dandelion (bal)
e.t.g. (fre)
eva restaurant (gl)
fu kun wu @ thaiku (bal)
hiroki (gl)
la carta oaxaca (bal)
le gourmand (bal)
persimmon (fre)
sambar (bal)
stumbling goat bistro (pr)

shop:
allusia (pr)
bark natural pet care (bal)
bellefleur lingerie (fre)
company k (fre)
lola pop (fre)
lucca great finds (bal)
lucca statuary (bal)
re-soul (bal)
souvenir (bal)

you can find the addresses and phone numbers for all of these businesses at our web-site: eatshopguides.com

if businesses that were fea-tured in a previous edition are not on this list, it means they have closed.

where to lay your weary head

there's many great places to stay in seattle, but here's a couple of kaie's picks:

hotel ändra
2000 fourth avenue
877.448.8600 / 206.448.8600
www.hotelandra.com
studio queen: $229
restaurant/bar: lola and assagio ristorante
notes: cocoon-comfortable modern rooms

the pan pacific seattle
2125 terry avenue
206.264.8111
www.panpacific.com/seattle
deluxe queen: $280.00
restaurant: marazul
notes: good location in the growing south lake union district, excellent service

the ace hotel
2423 first avenue
206.448.4721
www.acehotel.com
standard double with shared bath: $95 / king suite: $190. continental breakfast included
restaurant: cyclops downstairs, the macrina bakery across the street
notes: the chic hostel - affordable and stylish

pensione nichols
1923 first avenue
206.441.7125
www.pensionenichols.com
single occupancy: $98.00 suite: $230.00 breakfast included
restaurant: le pichet is just a couple of doors down!
notes: urban b&b with great views of the sound

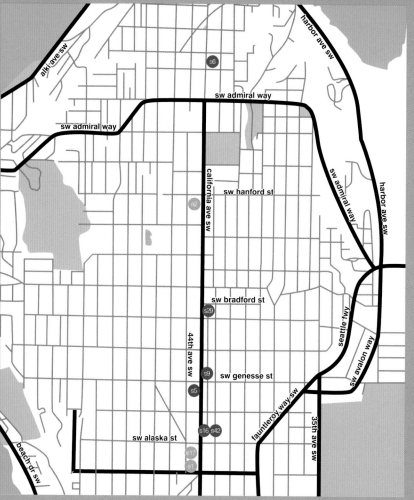

eat

e01 > bakery nouveau
e02 > beato food & wine
e17 > husky deli

shop

s05 > clementine
s06 > click! design that fits
s09 > divina
s16 > georgia blu
s29 > moxie papergoods & gifts
s42 > swee swee paperie & studio

west seattle

note: all maps face north

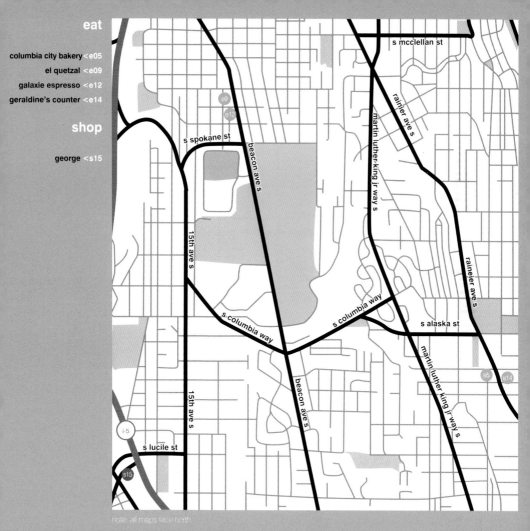

s mcclellan st

rainier ave s

martin luther king jr way s

s spokane st

beacon ave s

15th ave s

rainier ave s

s columbia way

s columbia way

s alaska st

martin luther king jr way s

beacon ave s

15th ave s

i-5

s lucile st

s15

note: all maps face north

columbia city / beacon hill / georgetown

eat

e24 > nielsen's pastries
e31 > steelhead diner
e32 > tavolata
e35 > vessel

shop

s08 > david smith & co
s11 > fancy pants
s22 > la rousse
s33 > oslo's
s34 > peter miller
s35 > polite society
s39 > rue
s40 > schmancy
s46 > tune
s47 > tuuli
s49 > urchin
s52 > watson kennedy

**belltown / pike place market / downtown /
south lake union / queen anne**

note: all maps face north

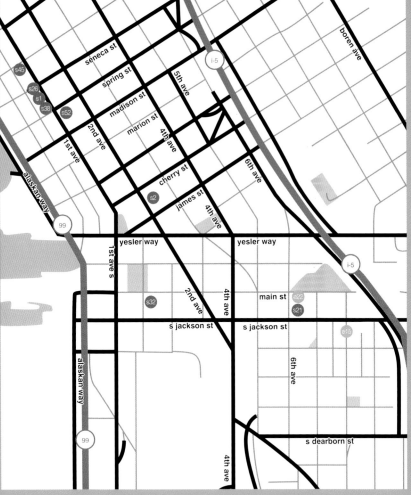

eat

green leaf <e15
maneki <e22

shop

a mano <s01
betty lin <s02
kobo <s21
maison luxe <s26
ornamo <s32
riveted <s38
tulip <s45
watson kennedy <s52

note: all maps face north

pioneer square / international district

fremont / phinney ridge / green lake / wallingford / ballard

note: all maps face north

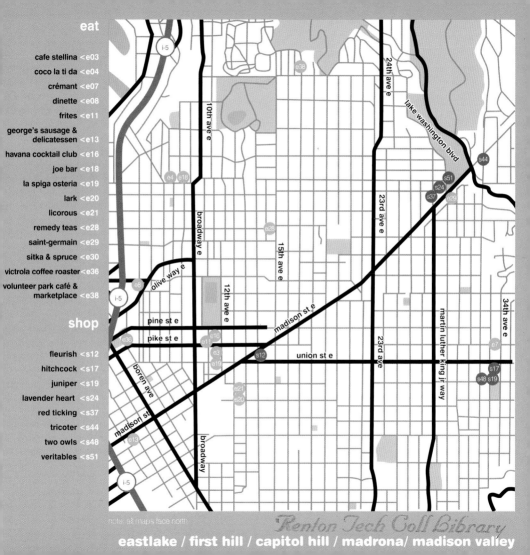

eat

cafe stellina <e03
coco la ti da <e04
crémant <e07
dinette <e08
frites <e11
george's sausage & delicatessen <e13
havana cocktail club <e16
joe bar <e18
la spiga osteria <e19
lark <e20
licorous <e21
remedy teas <e28
saint-germain <e29
sitka & spruce <e30
victrola coffee roaster <e36
volunteer park café & marketplace <e38

shop

fleurish <s12
hitchcock <s17
juniper <s19
lavender heart <s24
red ticking <s37
tricoter <s44
two owls <s48
veritables <s51

note: all maps face north

Renton Tech Coll Library

eastlake / first hill / capitol hill / madrona / madison valley

bakery nouveau

exquisite pastries, chocolate and more
4737 california avenue sw. at the alaskan junction
206.923.0534 www.bakerynouveau.com
mon - fri 6a - 7p sat 7a - 7p sun 7:30a - 6p

opened in 2007. owner / baker: william leaman
$: all major credit cards accepted
breakfast. lunch. treats. coffee/tea. bakery classes. first come, first served

west seattle >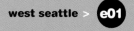

i love the the tagline of *bakery nouveau*: pastry. chocolate. bread. no need to use flowery language, because using just the basic nouns will get you into drool mode. most of west seattle has been frothing since william opened *bakery nouveau* earlier this year. from the moment i stepped foot on california avenue, i had both store owners and complete strangers literally walk me to the door. what thoughtful people. but what they didn't realize was i already had my highly attuned "delicious sweet things" radar on, and knew just where to aim.

imbibe / devour:
french press coffee
couverture hot chocolate
twice-baked almond croissant
pizza fresh from the oven
olive fougasse
chocolate banana tart
chocolate mousse raspberry
gorgeous chocolates

beàto food & wine

osteria and wine bar

3247 california avenue sw. between hines and hanford
206.923.1333 www.beatoseattle.com
tue - sun 5 - 11p

opened in 2007. owner: t. brandon gillespie chef: nick devine
$$ - $$$: all major credit cards accepted
dinner. reservations recommended

west seattle > 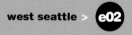 **e02**

lola is one of my favorite names in the world, which is why i gave it to my daughter. so in my book, anyplace that has a bartender named lola, is my type of place. *beàto's* lola is exactly who you would want to perch at a bar and chat with while eating meltingly tender veal short ribs and sipping from a flight of wine. sip, chat. bite, laugh. sip, sip and sip again. you get the idea. *beàto* could very well be one of those places where you might actually want to go solo, which for most people is unthinkable. but here, you've got instant friends.

imbibe / devour:
the weekly wine flight
menabrea beer
piatto misto
grilled zucchini tartufato
marinated onion & kumquat salad
beet gnocchi
braised veal short ribs
chocolate ravioli

cafe stellina

the next level of comfort food

1429 12th avenue, suite b. between madison and pike
206.322.2688
lunch mon - fri 11a - 3p dinner wed - sat 5 - 10p

opened in 2004. owners: teri esensten and mike cicon chef: terri esensten
$$: mc. visa
lunch. dinner. reservations accepted for 6 or more

capitol hill >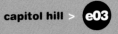

cafe stellina, *cafe stellina*, i do so love *cafe stellina*. i'm trying to make this into a song, but i'm stuck on just using the two words because they make me so happy. what is it about this place that tickles my food-ie bone? i think it's the utter lack of pretense. sure, there are white tablecloths and the food is knock-knockknockout. but if you look back at the kitchen, it's just teri cooking away on a couple of stoves that look like they were previously in your aunt mary's house. no chef this, and chef that. this place is proof that gorgeous food can come in a simple package.

imbibe / devour:
arco nova vinho verde
baked polenta, eggplant & crème fraiche
yam & peanut soup
angel hair pasta baked in parchment with
    french green beans & gorgonzola
chicken pot pie with rosemary gravy
pan-seared italian sausages with a lentil salad
lemon tart

coco la ti da

a sexy, sweet and savory lounge

806 east roy street. corner of broadway
206.789.2626 (COCO) www.cocolatida.com
tue - wed 5:30 - 10p thu - sat 5:30 - midnight sun 5:30 - 10p

opened in 2006. owner / chef: sue mccown
$ - $$: all major credit cards accepted
light dinner. treats. happy hour. late night. custom cakes, desserts and pastries
first come, first served

capitol hill >

i know you don't want me to tell you what to do, but i must suggest a perfect night out in seattle. grab a friend or beloved and take in a movie at the *harvard exit theater*. something weepy and dramatic will do, so by the end of the flick you must be resuscitated with a sweet jolt. and mercy me, right across the street from the theater is *coco la ti da*. my prescription: take your dessert in liquid form. the carrot cake liquid dessert will set your world right. still feeling a bit weak? there's a whole display case of temptations that will have you feeling good in no time.

imbibe / devour:
mother's little helper cocktail
carrot cake liquid dessert
savory lollipops
candy pork
the coco la ti da
bada bing bada boom
float me

columbia city bakery

beautiful breads and pastries

4865 rainier avenue south. between ferdinand and edmunds
206.723.6023
tue - fri 7a - 7p sat - sun 7a - 3p

opened in 2005. owner and baker: evan andres
$: mc. visa
breakfast. lunch. treats. coffee/tea. first come, first served

columbia city >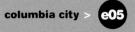

i am related to two pretzel-crazy people, my mother and my daughter. both would go berserk over the pretzels at *columbia city bakery* and would never desire a mushy mall pretzel again after eating the ones here. and there's a variety to choose from. there are the pretzel balls which could be fun to play a game of mini-boule with or butcher bob's pretzel dogs—the meal of champions. and take note, everything else here is world class which is why people who refuse to leave their own neighborhood have no problem crosstowning it to *columbia city* for their daily bread.

imbibe / devour:
macchiato
bostok
butcher bob's pretzel dog
seed ficelle
ginger cake with pears & maple mascarpone
   & pecan buttercream
apple morning bun
snowball
classic ham & brie sandwich

copper gate

legendary neighborhood bar with a new nordic twist

6301 24th avenue nw. corner of 63rd
206.706.2392 www.thecoppergate.com
daily 5p - midnight

opened in 1946. owner: heldig knut
chef: per amundsen   beverage overlord: perryn wright
$ - $$: all major credit cards accepted
dinner. full bar. happy hour from 5 - 7p   first come, first served

ballard >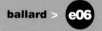

i don't know what's come over me, but i'm goofy for all things scan-di-noo-vian. maybe i've flown *s.a.s* one too many times, as i want to sip aquavit in a sauna while wearing nothing but a marimekko towel. hence why this book has a number of scandinavian-themed businesses, but none so outré as *copper gate*. until recently this was a favorite neighborhood dive, but then it got a bit of spiffing up and there are northern lovelies adorning the walls, cocktails from the mad liquor genius perryn, and the best swedish meatballs west of ikea. lyckliga dar!

imbibe / devour:
epple cider cocktail
kashk cocktail
long list of aquavits
sinebrychoff porter
spiced cauliflower soup
swedish meatballs
gravlax on pumpernickel
norwegian pancakes

crémant

cuisine traditionelle

1423 34th avenue. between pike and union
206.322.4600 www.cremantseattle.com
daily 5 - 11p

opened in 2006. owners: scott and tanya emerick chef: scott emerick
$$ - $$$: all major credit cards accepted
lunch. dinner. private dining. reservations recommended

madrona >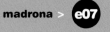

why am i fixated on foods that i can slather on bread? take paté for example. i deeply believe that spreadable meat is good for you. pair it with a slab of stinky, oozing cheese and this is french health food at its finest. at *crémant* the food is simple, traditional and ultimately french and this whole city is in love with it. and how could they not be? beyond the deeply satisfying food is one of the prettiest rooms in all of seattle with its dove gray walls and bright yellow door. *j'adore crémant.*

imbibe / devour:
poiré authentique
louis bouillot rosé
gratinée de halles
ouef en gelée au porto
gateaux de foie de volaille
petite salé
onglet de bouef
crème brûlée

dinette

rustic european fare

1514 east olive way. between howell and denny
206.328.2282 www.dinetteseattle.com
tue - sat open at 5:30p

opened in 2005. owner / chef: melissa nyffeler
$$: mc. visa
dinner. sunday supper. toast night on tuesday
reservations accepted for parties of 5 or more

capitol hill > **e08**

many people who profess to be in the food know in seattle love *dinette*. it's not because this place is some swank foodie temple; in fact, it's just the opposite. eating at *dinette* is like going to your best friend's house for dinner. in this case, your b.f. is melissa, and she's a whiz with toast. i'm not talking browned bread with a smear o' margarine. imagine instead perfectly crisped columbia city bakery bread with interesting savory combinations artfully arranged on top. but don't fill up on the bread only, because mel's menu is a poppin' with other delicious eats.

imbibe / devour:
white port cocktail
earl grey martini
the toast board:
  rabbit rillettes
  gorgonzola dolce
  smoked sardines & peperonata
handmade ricotta gnocchi
maker's mark bananas foster

el quetzal

authentic mexican homemade cuisine

3209 beacon hill south. between hanford and horton
206.329.2970
mon - sat 8a - 9p sun 8a - 4p

opened in 2006. owners: juan and helena montiel chef: juan montiel
$ - $$: mc. visa
breakfast. lunch. dinner. first come, first served

beacon hill > **e09**

i'm embarassed to admit that i have never been to mexico. well that's not exactly true, as i have been to tijuana. but in my mind, that doesn't count as the real mexico. i'm convinced tijuana is where americanized mexican cuisine was invented. so to savor the real cuisine of the country, you must get into the interior or you could go to *el quetzal* if your budget demands a road trip of fewer than ten miles. the food here truly gives a sense of what the authentic flavors of mexico are, and they are spectacular.

imbibe / devour:
sidral mundet
horchata
molletes
adobada rico tacos
super jairo gigante tortas
veggie norteno gigantes huaraches
pombazo's portales
el nopal salad

fresh flours

japanese-inspired bakery and café

6015 phinney avenue north. corner of 61st
206.297.3300 www.freshfloursseattle.com
mon - fri 6a - 5p sat - sun 7a - 5p

opened in 2005. owners: keiji koh and etsuko minematsu baker: keiji koh
$: mc. visa
breakfast. lunch. treats. coffee/tea. first come, first served

phinney ridge > **e10**

many years ago, i lived in tokyo for the summer. i look back now and wish that my unsophisticated teenage palate would have taken more chances with the japanese cuisine, but alas, ramen and japanese sweets were my staples. to this day, i have a soft spot for japanese treats, so *fresh flours* hits my sweet spot. this bakery is where japanese flavors fuse with western recipes, and the marriage is a delicious one. there's nobody else around who would dare combine kabocha pumpkin and white chocolate chips—it may sound wrong, but it's right in so many ways.

imbibe / devour:
green tea latte
blood orange & pear tea
kabocha pumpkin, pecan &
 white chocolate muffin
azuki cream brioche
savory pithivier
black sesame cookies
yuzu & cream soy pudding

frites

spot-on belgian frites
925 east pike. entrance on 10th
206.555.1212 www.belgianfrites.com
sun - thu 3p - midnight fri - sat 3p - 2:30a

opened in 2004. owners: corey allred and anthony falco
$: cash
dinner. late night. first come, first served

capitol hill > **e11**

in my pre-boring adult years, i would've given a small fortune to have had corey and anthony's belgian frites after a night of carousing. simply said, *frites* rocks. the night i visited, i wanted to order the super-size frites—the groot, just so i could say that word. but i controlled myself, and ordered the klein which was still a whopping cone of fried potato love. and which sauce to dip the frites in will tax even those who have retained full mind-power after a night of swilling. so i suggest, while still sober, make the sauce decision. corey and anthony will thank you for it.

imbibe / devour:
faygo original red pop
belgian frites in three sizes:
  klein, middel & groot
sauces:
  poblano ranch
  andalouse
  curry ketchup
gypsywurst

galaxie espresso

neighborhood beacon of calm and coffee
3215 beacon avenue south. between hanford and horton
206.860.7767 www.galaxieespresso.com
mon - fri 6:30a - 6p sat 7a - 6p sun 8a - 5p

opened in 2007. owners: yen banh and jeff woodward
$ - $$: mc. visa
breakfast. lunch. coffee/tea. first come, first served

beacon hill > **e12**

if any of you own the past editions of this guide, you'll know that i'm a big fan of siblings sophie and eric banh, who own *monsoon* and *bagutte box*. so when i heard that another banh sibling, yen, and her husband jeff, had opened a coffee house... i was there in a flash. *galaxie* anchors the south end of this charming little block in beacon hill and solidifies it as a small slice of foodie heaven as both *el quetzal* and *kusina filipina* are here also. start your day right at *galaxie* with a vietto and a *fresh flours* pastry—this tranquil space is the perfect respite from the city bustle.

imbibe / devour:
latte / mezzo
vietto (vietnamese coffee)
steamed cider
fresh flours pastries
baguette box sandwiches:
  prosciutto, goat cheese & fig
  braised tofu
  grilled yellow squash & eggplant

george's sausage & delicatessen

homemade smoked meats and deli
907 madison street. between 9th and terry
206.622.1491
mon - fri 9a - 5p sat 10a - 3p

opened in 1980. owner: janet lidzbarski
$ - $$: all major credit cards accepted
lunch. grocery. first come, first served

first hill >

in seattle there is a well-known cured meats mecca. i, like scads of other people, revere this place. but for those looking for a great alternative (and shorter lines), head to *george's*. this is the spot to come if you're hankering for some czech or polish style sausage—there must be at least a couple of dozen kinds, so close your eyes and take your pick. and while here, stock up on all of those eastern european foods that your larder has been lacking. janet will point out the essentials, all while making a truly gigantic deli sandwich for you.

imbibe / devour:
bull's blood of eger wine
mocny full beer
dozens of homemade czech-style sausages
big sandwiches made-to-order
e. wedel chocolates
andy's harvest & landbrot bread
sulguni cheese
assorted candies & cookies

geraldine's counter

comfort food in a sunny atmosphere

4872 rainier avenue south. corner of ferdinand
206.723.2080 www.geraldinescounter.com
tue - thu 7a - 9p fri 7a - 10p brunch sat - sun 8a - 3p

opened in 2005. owners: gary snyder and stacey hettinger chef: ramiro gallegos
$ - $$: mc. visa
breakfast. lunch. dinner. brunch. beer / wine. first come, first served

columbia city > e14

the day i went to *geraldine's counter*, i was a walking zombie. there were not enough eye drops in the world to soothe my scarily bloodshot eyes and i decided after slumping in my chair, i needed my mommy. since she wasn't readily available, i had to use *geraldine's* as a replacement, and the pineapple coffecake was the lovin' that i needed. i followed that up with the bacon, egg & arugula sandwich, and suddenly i had transformed from a whimpering shell of a person, to super-energized and refreshed kaie. this is the power of good comfort food.

imbibe / devour:
"devil made me do it" virgin mary
mac & jack's african amber beer
bacon, egg & arugula sandwich
sweet white corn, havarti & herb scramble
columbia city corned beef sandwich
chicken chutney salad
mama's meatloaf
beef stroganoff

green leaf

vietnamese restaurant
418 8th avenue south. corner of jackson
206.340.1388
daily 10:30a - 10p

opened in 2006 . owners: the kuang family chef: peter kuang
$ - $$: all major credit cards accepted
breakfast. lunch. dinner. catering. first come, first served

international district > e15

often when i'm working on these guides, i visit both eating and shopping places so i never go hungry. but one day in seattle i found myself just shopping. around the three p.m. hour i began to feel a gurgling nauseous feeling. what was this feeling? unexpected pregnancy? shopping delirium? noooo, it was a deep, desperate hunger. i raced like a starving banshee to *green leaf* and ordered enough food for me and my four invisible friends. and what a feast "we" had. this is vietnamese cuisine at its best and it's even better when served by the friendliest staff in town.

imbibe / devour:
soda sua hot ga (egg soda)
soda chanh muoi (pickled lemondade soda)
banh tam bi (rice noodle with coconut sauce)
banh xeo (vietnamese pancake)
goi ngo sen (lotus root salad)
hu tieu my tho (my tho noodles)
mi vit tiem (fried duck noodle soup)
banh nep chuoi nuong (grilled banana cake)

havana cocktail club

cuban style speakeasy with a modern twist
1010 east pike street. between 10th and 11th (enter in the parking lot)
206.323.CUBA (2822) www.havanasocial.com
daily 4p - 2a

opened in 2006. owner: quentin ertel
$: all major credit cards accepted
full bar. happy hour. first come, first served

capitol hill >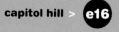

seattle is a bar town. walk a block or two, and there will be a bar. some are great, and some are of the "i'll take the two-for-one bud light" variety. quentin has been involved with some of the great ones, so there was a good chance when he opened *havana cocktail club*, that it would be a knockout. it is. the drinks are old-school and go down smoothly, and there's plenty of dark seductive nooks that invite a bit o' snogging. only thing not supplied is the snogging partner—that you'll need to find yourself.

imbibe:
cocktails:
  paper tiger
  el floridita
  royal palm
  hotel st. george
  nacional
  yokohama romance

43

husky deli

beloved family owned west seattle grocery and delicatessen

4721 california avenue sw. at the alaskan junction
206.937.2810 www.huskydeli.com
mon - sat 9a - 9p sun 10a - 7p

opened in 1932. owner: jack miller
$ - $$: all major credit cards accepted
grocery. catering. delivery. first come, first served

west seattle > e17

the *husky deli* is a landmark in west seattle. zillions of kids have come here since 1932 to get their ice-cream fix while their parents stocked up on fresh deli items and groceries. shopping here today is like hopping on a bus to europe and the british isles. need a jar of marmite and some tinned sprats? get 'em here. and note, if you can't find your child at the ice-cream counter, don't fret, as he/she's guaranteed to be trolling the candy area which seems to have a tractor beam attached to it. my basket runneth over.

imbibe / devour:
fess parker's frontier red wine
husky ice cream:
  licorice & french orange
  husky flake
turkish delight sandwich
great selection of english & scandinavian foods
ski queen gjetost cheese
candy, candy, candy

joe bar

have a crêpe with your coffee
810 east roy. corner of broadway
206.324.0407 www.joebar.org
mon - fri 7:30a - 9:30p sat - sun 8:30a - 9:30p

opened in 1997. owner: wylie bush
$: mc. visa
breakfast. lunch. dinner. coffee/tea. wine/beer. first come, first served

capitol hill > **e18**

devon and eric are my new best friends. they work at *joe bar*. devon is the masta barista, and eric the crêpe king. together, they form a dynamic duo. watching them in action is impressive. even when a line began to form, as it does here often because seattleites are crazy about this place, devon kept everyone (does he know the whole city by name?) happy, and served in a jiffy. but the supreme happiness here is the nutella crêpe. what makes it so good is the magic dusting of cinnamon sugar. happy happy happy.

imbibe / devour:
good cuppa joe
winter: gluhwein / summer: lillet
crêpes:
  smoked salmon, kale, bleu cheese & chives
  nutella, cinnamon sugar & whip
salami, gruyère & roasted red pepper panini
spinach, tomato & peppered chevre salad
carne y queso plate

la spiga osteria

authentic cuisine from the emilia-romagna region of italy

1429 12th avenue, suite b. corner of pike
206.323.8881 www.laspiga.com
dinner daily 5 - 11p   bar menu from 11p - 1:30a

opened in 1998. owners: pietro borghesi and sabrina tinsley chef: sabrina tinsley
$$ - $$$: all major credit cards accepted
dinner. full bar. wine/beer. reservations recommended

capitol hill > **e19**

over the last decade, i have spent a fair amount of time in northern italy. and though i've eaten the cuisine from this region stateside, nothing has quite matched up to the real thing. then i sat down to a big bowl of tagliatelle al ragu at *la spiga osteria*. it was perfection in a dish. careful preparation + simple, beautifully sourced ingredients = eating satisfaction. this is the fail-proof formula that makes the cuisine of emilia-romagna so desirable and why *la spiga*, in its swanky new space, continues to be a food-lover's destination.

imbibe / devour:
basiico cocktail
sforzato di valtellina san domenico 2001
tagliatelle al ragu
mortadella alla griglia
sformato di fossa con saba
stracotto alla parmigiana
zucca arrosto
panna cotta agli agrumi

lark

cuisine featuring sustainable products sourced from trusted artisans

926 12th avenue. between spring and marion
206.323.5275 www.larkseattle.com
tue - sun 5 - 10:30p

opened in 2003. owners: john sundstrom, kelly ronan and jim enos
chef: john sundstrom
$$ - $$$: mc. visa
dinner. full bar. reservations accepted for parties of six or more

capitol hill > **e20**

lark was a revelation to seattle diners when it opened a couple years back, and people talked about it across state lines. from the first time i visited, i've contemplated what elements make *lark* special and i've concluded that what puts it on a higher plane is its perfect balance. the yin and the yang here is palpable with the pairing of exquisitely prepared and sourced food and the soothing atmosphere. with this balance should come a good appetite. though the menu is a fine read, it's an even better eat.

imbibe / devour:
rhubarb dry soda
cantina del pino "ovello" barbaresco '01
pear & mizuna salad with
  brick pastry & wrapped chèvre
lomo with 12th century chutney
roasted eel with saba & new potato salad
goose confit tart with
  hedgehog mushrooms & cream
coconut sorbet with champagne mango

licorous

tempting the appetite

928 12th avenue south. nearest cross street is madison
206.325.6947 www.licorous.com
tue - sat 5p - 1a

opened in 2006
owners: tim johnstone, michelle magidow, john sundstrom and kelly ronan
chef: gordon wishard, jr.
$$: mc. visa
light dinner. full bar. first come, first served

capitol hill >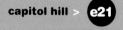

next door to *lark*, is its younger sibling, *licorous*. this is where you come when you're not feeling like a big meal, but a drink and a nibble or two, or in my case, three or four. the poached egg sandwich was, to my hungry eyes, the most beautiful plate of food i'd ever seen. i fell upon it like a bear coming out of hibernation and i think i might have licked my chops after finishing. once done devouring, i turned my attention to libating. the cocktails here are smartly conceived and use *licorous's* house-infused liquors, and they go down the gullet quite easily. happy sigh.

imbibe / devour:
the lark cocktail
the langue du chat cocktail
the caribbean pepper nib cocktail
foie gras bon bons
braised venison tartine
tuna crudo
poached egg sandwich
brown butter-hazelnut financiers

maneki

authentic japanese cuisine
304 6th avenue south. between main and jackson
206.622.2631 www.manekirestaurant.com
tue - sun 5:30 - 10:30p

opened in 1904. owner: jean nakayama
$$: all major credit cards accepted
dinner. full bar. tatami rooms. reservations recommended

international district > e22

when you're writing a book about local businesses, there's always a small fear whether the business will be able to buck the trend and stay open for more than a year. i would say that *maneki*, which has been in business for a paltry 103 years, is going to make it. though it's changed locations and owners a couple of times over the last century, it's not changed its loyal fan base. jean knows most of the customers by name, and after spending the evening talking to her and eating intensely satisfying japanese comfort food, i was the newest card-carrying member of the fan club.

imbibe / devour:
kentaro cockatil
junmai nigori sayuri sake
spicy tuna bata-yaki
yamaimo sengiri
oyster miso rockefeller
ankimo
beautiful sushi
maneki ice supreme

mighty-o donuts

donuts that are good for you!

2110 north 55th street. corner of keystone
206.547.0335 www.mightyo.com
mon - tue 6a - noon wed - sat 6a - 5p sun 7a - 5p

opened in 2003. owner: ryan kellner
$: mc. visa
treats. coffee/tea. first come, first served

green lake > e23

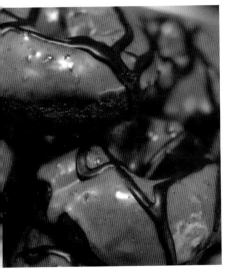

here's a short laundry list of why *mighty-o donuts* are beneficial to your health and well-being. there's no trans-fats used and they are organic, vegan and dairy free. the only thing missing is fat-free. don't worry— the latest studies done by my crack team of under-eight-year-old scientists prove that donut fat is one of the good types of fat. not only are these donuts better for you to consume, but they are also pretty to look at. big stacks of chocolate donuts glazed with pink icing and drizzled with chocolate—say cheese, you pretty little circles of deliciousness.

imbibe / devour:
cold milk in a mug
mocha made with homemade chocolate syrup
donuts:
  grasshopper
  french toast
  cuckoo for coconut
  nutty chocolate
  glazed

nielsen's pastries

traditional danish bakery

520 2nd avenue west. corner of mercer
206.282.3004 www.nielsenspastries.com
mon 7:30a - 3p tue - fri 7:30a - 5:30p sat 8a - 3p

opened in 1965. owner / chef: darcy person
$: mc. visa
lunch. treats. coffee/tea. first come, first served

lower queen anne > **e24**

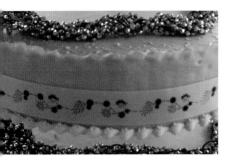

sometimes you meet a person and you realize that the person is the other you because they eerily look or talk like you. my doppelganger is anna whom i met at *polite society*. not only do we look and dress alike, but our true connection is that we both deeply love old-school bakeries. when anna shared with me her passion for *nielsen's pastries* and their snitters one evening, i had snittery dreams all night long. by eight a.m. the next day, i had a snitter in hand. and then a kringle. i couldn't stop myself. i was in special type of pastry delirium, and i've yet to recover.

imbibe / devour:
hot tea or coffee
snitters
kringles
potatoes (pastry)
napoleon hats
marzipan wedding cakes
kransekages
good sandwiches

oliver's twist

drink + eat + more
6822 greenwood avenue north. corner of 70th
206.706.MORE (6673) www.oliverstwistseattle.com
mon - sat 5p - 1a

opened in 2006. owners: dan braun and sarah hughes-giles chef: dan braun
$$: mc. visa
dinner. full bar. first come, first served

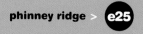

phinney ridge > **e25**

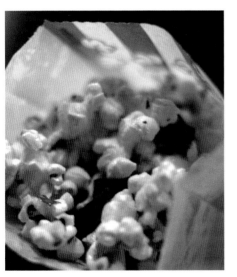

my father makes the world's most delicious popcorn. he pops a big kettle of corn, pours melted butter over it and then grates cheddar cheese on top. i'm salivating at the thought. but dan might have topped my dad's culinary masterpiece with his garlic truffled popcorn, not only because it's aromatically delightful, but it comes in a groovy popcorn bag. you see this whimsy everywhere at *oliver's twist*, from the cocktails that are like no other's in town, to the unexpected pairings of textures and flavors on the menu. even fagin would crack a smile.

imbibe / devour:
old sally cocktail
artful dodger cocktail
garlic truffled popcorn
lamb prosciutto, melon & mint flower honey
blue cheese, bacon-stuffed dates &
  marcona almonds
peanut butter caramel & chocolate gelato
  with sea salt

olsen's scandinavian foods

the west coast's largest scandinavian food store

2248 nw market street. between 22nd and 24th
206.783.8288 www.scandinavianfoods.net
mon - fri 9a - 5p sat 10a - 5p

opened in 1960. owners: anita and reidun endresen
$ - $$: mc. visa
grocery. first come, first served

ballard >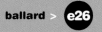

if you took a gander in my fridge, you would find an entire section dedicated to mustard—and there are probably a dozen more jars waiting in my pantry for their moment of glory. one of my favorite places to buy mustard is *olsen's scandinavian foods*. i love the idun brand mustards with the circa '70s squeezable bottle. mustard not your thing? you could pick up instead a copy of *91 ways to serve lefse* or a couple of trolls. top off your basket with some of *olsen's* famous meatballs, some flatbreads and finnish black licorice, and away you go!

imbibe / devour:
olsen's homemade meatballs
mors flatbread
kavli original cheese spread
whole sprats of anchovy
idun mustard in the squeeze bottle
finnska soft licorice
tomte glogg
trolls!

paseo caribbean

seattle loves this joint

4225 fremont avenue north. between 42nd and 43rd
206.545.7440 www.nowebsite.com
tue - sat 11:30a - 9p

opened in 1995. owner / chef: lorenzo lorenzo
$ - $$: cash
lunch. dinner. first come, first served

fremont >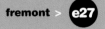

there's only one reason people form a line outside of a restaurant in seattle on a spongy-wet day. no, they're not queuing up for the toilet or waiting while rachel ray and her crew film a spot. at *paseo*, the line is for *the* sandwich. it's the 'wich that's been blogged about from kirkland to kelso—the midnight cuban. i'd driven by the line at the miniscule hut in fremont for years, chortling away that i would not be seduced by the cuban. but for some reason on a recent, grotty-grey day, i broke down. and yes, dammit—the sandwich is all that. but the smokin' thighs were even more…

imbibe / devour:
a cold coke
sandwiches:
  midnight cuban
  sautéed prawns
  havana seared scallops
smokin' thighs platter
west caribbean bowl
cuban roast plato

remedy teas

a fresh, modern organic tea café

345 15th avenue east. entrance on harrison
206.323.4TEA (4832) www.remedyteas.com
daily 7a - 11p

opened in 2006. owners: anthony, andrea and chris arnold
$: all major credit cards accepted
breakfast. lunch. treats. tea. some alcoholic beverages. first come, first served

capitol hill > e28

way before the experts were expounding on tea's health benefits, i was convinced drinking it daily would make me taller, wiser and my thin hair fuller. from india to france to morocco, i searched for the most unusual varieties—but now i need go no further than *remedy teas*. the scope and quality of tea here is breathtaking. if you need to know how many different types anthony stocks, just look to the numbered containers on the front wall—i thought i would faint from tea ecstasy. but i stayed upright to try the uniquely fantastic creations anthony makes with his teas... swoon.

imbibe / devour:
rooibos chai latte
green vitality smoothie
citra mate sake
matcha mojito
"the works" tea service (also for kids)
beautiful cheese plate
toast & jam
tea-infused truffles

67

saint-germain

bistro and winebar

2811a east madison street. corner of 28th
206.323.9800 www.saintgermainseattle.com
tue - thu 11a - midnight fri - sat 11 - 2a

opened in 2006. owner: jean-michel omnés
$$: all major credit cards accepted
lunch. dinner. wine/beer. first come, first served

madison valley > **e29**

the first time i went to paris, i was seventeen years old, and i stayed in a tiny hotel room in the latin quarter with my brother david. some of my crystal clear memories from that trip include eating in the small cafés of the arrondissement. there was nothing pretentious about the food served, but it was always delectable. *saint-germain* has the same feeling. the food here is rustic and simple, from a savory tartine to a crisp salade niçoise. and the strolling guitarist who looks like a parisian busker? that's jean-michel the owner doing double-duty.

imbibe / devour:
boizel rosé
assiette de fromages
tartines:
    monsieur seguin
    la paysanne
salade niçoise
endives au jambon gratin
poires belle-hélène

sitka & spruce

honest food with an inventive twist

2238 eastlake avenue east. between lynn and boston
206.324.0662 www.sitkaandspruce.com
lunch tue - fri 11:30a - 1:30p
dinner wed - sat 5:30 - 10:30p sunday supper 6:30p / 8:30p

opened in 2006. owner/chef: matthew dillon
$$ - $$$: all major credit cards accepted
lunch. dinner. wine/beer. reservations accepted for parties of five or more

eastlake > **e30**

yes, this restaurant is in a strip mall, as is often pointed out in the press. but with that said, it doesn't matter where *sitka & spruce* is located. the interesting story here is the food. the agenda is simple: source über-fresh, locally grown ingredients and create a new menu daily to show them off. all this is done without an ounce of pomp, but with some glorious circumstance. matt falls into that special breed of chefs that is not so much interested in the glory, but in the craft, and that's refreshing.

imbibe / devour:
carrots in dill
fluke tartare, castelveltrano olives & mint
semolina gnocci, stinging nettles & ricotta
squab breast, prunes & fresca sarda
black pig rib chops, piquillos & pimenton
lobster, vanilla & grilled escarole
potatoes braised in cream
crêpes with orange marmalade & ricotta

steelhead diner

upmarket northwest diner with a southern twist

95 pine street, suite #17. corner of 1st avenue
206.625.0129 www.steelheaddiner.com
tue - fri 11:30a - 10p sat 10a - 10p sun 10a - 5p

opened in 2007. owners: kevin and terresa davis chef: kevin davis
$$: all major credit cards accepted
lunch. dinner. brunch. full bar. reservations accepted

pike place market > **e31**

you gotta love a fly-fishin', louisiana boy who ends up in seattle. kevin has circumnavigated the globe, cooking up a storm, but now he's anchored himself in seattle with the *steelhead diner*. kevin makes what i would term hybrid, regionally-inspired comfort food. what's that mean exactly? good food, people... good food. the crabcake is outrageous, there must be the meat of a whole crab in the cake. pair it up with a gumbo that's got the perfect amount of heat, and a local brew—oooweee, that's some good eats.

imbibe / devour:
emerald city green tea cocktail
alaska stout
caviar pie
jumbo lump dungeness crab cake
"rich-boy" with uli's hot sausage
slow-braised washington beef short ribs
ligurian lemon cake
annel's candies

73

tavolàta

un-pretentious italian cuisine

2323 second avenue. between battery and bell
206.838.8008 www.tavolata.com
daily 5p - 1a

opened in 2007. owners: ethan stowell and patric gabre-kidan chef: ethan stowell
$$: all major credit cards accepted
dinner. full bar. reservations accepted for parties of six or more

belltown >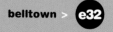

i know you're all waiting to hear whether or not ethan remains the sexiest chef in seattle. if the vote was based on his new restaurant, *tavolàta*, then applause (please ladies, no throwing of undergarments)—his reign continues. *union*, his first and still going strong restaurant, is all about craft and precision. *tavolàta* is about simplicity and passion. after some prosecco, broiled oysters and the t-bone for two, you'll be feeling the love. as for me, i want to sleep on the scrumptious pillow-like zeppole. sweet dreams.

imbibe / devour:
adami garbel prosecco
marchesi di gresy 'martinenga' nebbiolo langhe
veal carpaccio
broiled oysters
spaghetti with anchovies, garlic & red chili
fried ricotta gnocchi
two-person grilled t-bone
zeppole

75

35th street bistro

country european cuisine
709 north 35th street. corner of fremont
206.547.9850 www.35bistro.com
mon 5 - 11p tue - sun 11a - 11p

opened in 2002. owner: bob day chef: steve smrstik
$$: all major credit cards accepted
lunch. dinner. brunch. full bar. reservations recommended

fremont >

i am partial to eating; hence, i author books about it. i will admit though, that after i've finished doing the research and photography for a city, i'm tempted to fast until the next city. this always sounds good, but my fasts last about ten minutes and then i start dreaming of food. when i've fallen off the depravation wagon, *35th street bistro* is just the ticket. the european-style fare here will whet any appetite. but beware of entering with an empty stomach, as the smells coming from the kitchen will make you weep in hungry anticipation.

imbibe / devour:
black cherry bellini
foss marai prosecco
bistro frites
prosciutto & manchego sandwich
crêpes aubergines
boudin blanc
goat cheese & caramelized onion ravioli
pear & almond pithivier

trophy cupcakes and party

festive treats and goods

1815 north 45th street, suite #209. in the wallingford center
206.632.7020 www.trophycupcakes.com
mon - fri 6:30a - 8p sat 8:30a - 6p sun 8:30a - 8p

opened in 2007. owner / baker: jennifer shea
$ - $$: mc. visa
treats. coffee/tea. custom orders. first come, first served

wallingford >

have you ever wondered what the secret is to getting kids to behave in a car? here's the answer: you take a minivan and fill it with six kids post school. you then open a box filled with *trophy cupcakes* to a round of oohs and aahs. i guarantee all rules of conduct will be complied with asap, just to have the chance to devour one of jennifer's pretty, pretty cupcakes. the problem though, is that the cupcakes are sooo appealing that the poppets can't decide which to have. i sympathize with this dilemma.

imbibe / devour:
thick, european hot chocolate
french soda
cupcakes:
  lemon strawberry
  peanut butter & jelly
  green tea
covet:
pretty paper goods & party supplies

vessel

urban chic bar

1312 fifth avenue. between university and union
206.963.9657 www.vesselseattle.com
mon - fri 11:30a - close sat - sun 4p - close

opened in 2006. owners: coleman c. johnson and clark c. niemeyer
drink designer: jamie boudreau chef: dawn fornear
$$: all major credit cards accepted
lunch. dinner. full bar. first come, first served

downtown > e35

i'm a sucker for a pretty drink. i'm not talking the mai tai with an umbrella variety, but the type that has some serious inspiration behind it. the vessel 75 is a drink to lust for. take a bit of top-drawer bourbon, a splash of bitters and a dollop of maple-syrup foam on top and voilà—pretty personified. take this drink and place it in a gorgeous room, and you have *vessel*. this is big-city cocktailing with a bit of healthy attitude that will make you feel like taking off your stodgy, weather-proof shoes, and slipping into some sultry heels and a sexy little something.

imbibe / devour:
cocktails:
  vessel 75
  frick
  naramata
  chrysanthemum
wilted escarole with duck egg
croque monsieur petit sandwiches
truffles

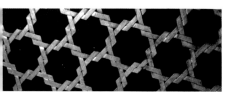

victrola coffee roasters

passionate coffee for those who believe

café and roastery: 310 east pike street between melrose and bellevue. 206.624.1725
coffee and art: 411 15th avenue east. between aloha and thomas. 206.325.6520
www.victrolacoffee.net
daily 5:30a - 11p

opened in 2000. owners: jen strongin and chris sharp
$: all major credit cards accepted
coffee/tea. light fare. treats. first come, first served

capitol hill >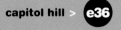

the new *victrola café and roastery* on pike feels reverent—the morning i was there jesus beams shot through the big windows and some nearby angels were egging me on to drink full caf coffee. this must be heaven. at *victrola*, there are followers aplenty. in a town where bad coffee might be legislated as a crime, *victrola's* rises to celestial heights because they source the finest beans and roast them in house, which means that your delicious cuppa joe here is going to radiate with freshness.

imbibe / devour:
coffee:
  empire blend (drip)
  streamline (espresso)
  ethiopian harrar
  sumatra gayo mountain
a french press of coffee
serendipitea burrough's brew
delish baked goods

volterra

contemporary italian

5411 ballard avenue nw. corner of 22nd
206.789.5100 www.volterrarestaurant.com
mon - thu 5p - midnight fri 5p - 1a sat-sun brunch 9a - 2p dinner 5p - 1a

opened in 2005. owners: don curtiss and michelle quisenberry chef: don curtiss
$$ - $$$: all major credit cards accepted
dinner. brunch. full bar. reservations recommended

ballard >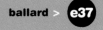

everybody has an opinion about what their favorite restaurant is in seattle. i know because i pose this question to just about everyone i meet. one restaurant that inspired a lot of love from the committed diner-outers of seattle was *volterra*. from day one, this restaurant was embraced not only by the ballard locals, but also by a wide swath of the city. the earthy, tuscan cuisine is the draw—it's inspired by don and michelle's numerous stays in the region. so if a trip to italy is not in the cards, just rent *stealing beauty* and then eat at *volterra* and get a bit of la dolce vita.

imbibe / devour:
white pear cosmo
avignonesi vino nobile di montepulciano 2002
piatto di formaggi
pork jowls & lentil salad
sausage & saluggia bean risotto
beef cheek ravioli
tuscan beef stew
cherry & chocolate glace

volunteer park cafe & marketplace

always fresh goodness

1501 17th avenue east. corner of galer
206.328.3155 www.alwaysfreshgoodness.com
tue - fri 7a - 5p sat - sun 8a - 5p

opened in 2007. owner/chefs: ericka burke (savory) and heather earnhardt (sweet)
$ - $$: mc. visa
breakfast. lunch. treats. coffee/tea. small grocery. first come, first served

capitol hill > **e38**

volunteer park cafe & marketplace is the perfect tucked-away gem. when seattle is grey and glum, this little neighborhood café will always be warm and yellow and sunny. feeling a little sniffly and low? no need to dose yourself with kava and echinacea; the better medicine would be to come here, snuggle up in a corner with a good book, have some soothing soup, then a bit of tea to go with volunteer's crinkle cookies that are just like your grandmother made. see now, don't you feel better?

imbibe / devour:
pear-ginger lemonade
volunteer park hot chocolate
warm hazelnut-crusted chevre salad
brie & apple panini
caramelized banana brioche french bread
four cheese panini & tomato bisque
orange chocolate bundt cake
chocolate crinkle cookies

kaie's twenty favorite things

01 > baked polenta, eggplant & crème fraiche at cafe stellina

02 > swedish meatballs at copper gate

03 > kabocha pumpkin, pecan & white chocolate muffin at fresh flours

04 > prosciutto, goat cheese & fig baguette at galaxie espress

05 > banh tam bi at green leaf

06 > nutella, cinnamon sugar & whip crepe at joe bar

07 > poached egg sandwich at licorous

08 > spicy tuna bata-yaki at maneki

09 > citra mate sake at remedy teas

10 > vessel 75 at vessel

11 > alexander mcqueen gilded stilettos at betty lin

12 > javanese teahouse at david smith & co

13 > timorous beasties wallpaper at ornamo

14 > subversive jewelry necklace at hitchcock

15 > tsumori chisato everything at impulse

16 > wolfette ring at kimberly baker jewelry

17 > hakusan rock handle mugs at kobo

18 > ports 1961 everything at merge

19 > aaron murray animal figurines & shadow boxes at nancy

20 > salvaged 15' cedar table at okok

eat

shop

a mano

beautifully crafted shoes and accessories

1115 first avenue. between spring and seneca
206.292.1767 www.shopamano.com
mon - sat 10a - 6p sun noon - 5p

opened in 2006. owner: nealy blau
all major credit cards accepted
online shopping

almost pioneer square > **s01**

for many years, a shopping trip to first avenue meant a stop at *ped* to buy shoes. and then last year, dayna closed *ped's* storefront to focus on cyber-selling. seattle (and well-beyond) shoe lovers mourned the loss, but they didn't need to for long. nealy, who had worked at *ped* for years, took over the space and named her new venture *a mano*. while the spirit of *ped* lives on and some of the same beloved lines found there are represented, *a mano* has its own voice and style. long live *a mano*.

covet:
shoes:
  fiorentini & baker
  chie mahara
  moma
  miho masui
  cydwoq
jamie joseph jewelry
sarah mcquire jewelry

betty lin

designer off-price clothing and shoes (but not off the mark!)

608 2nd avenue. between james and cherry
206.442.6888 www.shopbettylin.com
mon - sat 10a - 6p

opened in 2005. owner: betty lin
all major credit cards accepted
online shopping

almost pioneer square > 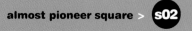 **s02**

the first couple of times i visited *betty lin* (formerly *betty blue*), i was overwhelmed. the store was packed with off-price designer clothing and shoes, and my mind couldn't grasp where to begin. then i met betty. as i was combing through the shoe racks, gurgling with pleasure over a guilded pair of alexander mc-queen stilletos, betty quickly discerned my likes and dislikes. she then guided me to the racks and pulled out glorious pieces by yohji, alaia and more. i could have hugged her, and i think many customers do. by the time you leave here, betty will be a friend for life.

covet:
comme des garçons
yohji yamamoto
rick owens
kenneth jay lane
azzedine alaia
lanvin
aristolasia bags
shoe collection that will make you weep

bitters co.

eclectic general store

513 north 36th street. corner of dayton
206.632.0886 www.bittersco.com
tue - sat 11a - 6p sun noon - 5p

opened in 1993. owners: katie and amy carson
mc. visa
online shopping. gift registries. custom orders / design

fremont > **s03**

since i started doing these books, i've noticed a growing change in the world of retail. i began to see a number of stores carrying sustainably produced, fair-trade goods. some places might just now be jumping on the bandwagon (good!), but *bitters co.* has been walking the talk for well over a decade. the sisters carson source goods from around the world, and even their own backyard, where amy keeps a studio. here she creates simple, beautifully crafted products out of reclaimed wood so each has a rich patina. you can feel the care.

covet:
amy carson sculpted stools & other designs
mexican tin trucks
marni turkel ceramics
abaca striped knapsacks
cork birdhouses
heath ceramics
cast bronze house numbers from ghana
saturn press cards

blackbird

men's clothing & effects

5410 22nd avenue nw. between ballard and market
206.547.2524 helloblackbird.blogspot.com
mon - fri 9a - 8p sat 9a - 9p sun 9a - 7p

opened in 2004. owners: nicole miller and scott dierdorf
mc. visa
online shopping

ballard >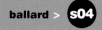

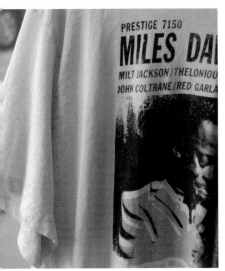

i've always secretly admired blackbirds. though my mother has trained my daughter to race after them and bellow, "shoo blackbird, shoo," i find these birds handsome with their glossy black feathers and bold voices. so *blackbird*, the store, is aptly named. nicole has made bold buying choices with the men's clothing and accoutrements since the day she opened, and the guys in seattle have been the better for it. she's taken the classic seattle style and urbanized it… an effect that's totally modern, and yet utterly distinctive.

covet:
nom de guerre
surface to air
cheap monday
b. son
filippa k
rvca
a.p.c.
baxter of california

clementine

funky, fun mix of shoes and accessories

4447 california avenue sw. between oregon and genesee
206.935.9400 www.clementines.com
tue - fri 11a - 7p sat 10a - 6p sun 11a - 5p

opened in 2006. owner: linda walsh
mc. visa
online shopping

west seattle >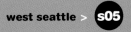

at this point, i think it would be safe to say that most women i know are shoe junkies. though i think there are different levels of addiction. i would put myself at a pretty serious, might need help level. i'm not just into any, old shoe. i look for what i call personality shoes. the type that you put on and everyone you meet asks where you got them. *clementine* carries shoes like this. the malole wedge that's shown in the main picture here, would turn heads from portland to paris—it's that pretty. drats, why didn't i buy a pair?

covet:
shoes:
  maloles
  glory chen
  giraudon
  sam edelman
  lundi bleu
  salpy
chemical wedding bags

click! design that fits

contemporary home furnishings and personal accessories

2210 california avenue sw. one block north of admiral
206.328.9252 www.clickdesignthatfits.com
tue - fri noon - 7p sat - sun 11a - 5p

opened in 2004. owners: john and frances smersh
mc. visa
online shopping. gift registries

west seattle > **s06**

when i first heard the name of this store, it took me a second to process its meaning. then the ah-hah came and i realized that *click! design that fits* makes complete sense, not only as a store, but also as a mantra. sometimes in this world of too much, we just buy things to fill space. but at *click!*, you'll find beautifully designed products that make sense, that are useful and are not just wanted, but needed. craft is of the essence to john and frances, and you'll find it in abundance here.

covet:
smersh design concrete, pearls & cork jewelry
julie burton & jess panzl glass bottles
josh jakus felt bags
urbancase made-to-order furniture
rotating 2-d art
eva zeisel for klein reid creamer/sugar set
wingard clocks
angela adams bags

101

clover

unique and magical toys, furniture and clothing for children

5335 ballard avenue nw. between 22nd and vernon
206.782.0715 www.clovertoys.com
mon - sat 10a - 6p sun 10a - 5p

opened in 2004. owner: sarah furstenberg
all major credit cards accepted
gift registries. custom orders / design

ballard >

it's interesting to me to watch the progression of what toys my six-year-old daughter lola wants to play with. when *clover* first opened, lola was four, and she was enthralled with playing dress-up. by five, she wanted to collect animal figurines and now at six, it's a toss up between stuffed animals and dolls. *clover* has been able to fulfill all of lola's toy desires through each of these phases and will continue to do so probably until she's fully-grown up, as we adults like the goodies here just as much as the kiddos do.

david smith & co

artisan created furniture and antiques from southeast asia

1107 harrison street. corner of fairview
206.223.1598 www.davidsmithco.com
daily 11a - 6p

opened in 1989. owner: david smith
all major credit cards accepted
custom orders / design

south lake union > **s08**

my husband and i constantly talk about purchasing a new bed—it's part of our furniture fantasy talk. the bed we discuss is modern, but what i secretly yearn for is the extraordinary chinese wedding bed at *david smith & co*. this is the grown-up version of the princess bed, as you couldn't help but feel regal slumbering in this ornate piece. we also have a landscaping fantasy, where our backyard becomes an oasis of calm. here we can use david's teak garden furniture. and so i have a place for my morning beverage, i'll take one javanese teahouse, please.

covet:
joglo hand-carved structure
javanese teahouse
teak garden furniture
stone mortar planters
krupuk tins
java wood chips
magical chinese clocks
tade cluster sphere lamps

divina

saving the world one piece of art at a time

4160 california avenue sw. corner of genesee
206.938.9388 www.divinaseattle.com
hours are seasonal, see website

opened in 2006. owner: julie mirielle anderson
mc. visa
online shopping. art classes

west seattle >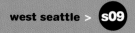

when searching for businesses to feature in this book, the first thing i look for is passion. i want to feel the owner's zeal for what he/she does from the moment i walk in their front door. *divina* is a great example of this. what drew me in here were the spectacular, chunky knit sweaters and dresses. their beauty captured me, but the craft inspired me. julie develops close relationships with latin american artisans, so she can support and nurture these craftspeople and purchase their goods at fair-market prices. this is global commerce at its finest.

covet:
divina hand-crafted uruguan wool clothing
manos del uruguay sagali handbags
veronica artagaveytia jewelry
maria jose jewelry
joaquin torres garcia skill games
various artisan products
pewter shot glasses
handmade books

essenza

luscious mix of beauty products, lingerie and infant wear

615 north 35th street. between evanston and fremont
206.547.4895 www.essenzaseattle.com
mon - wed 11a - 6p thu - sat 11a - 7p sun 11a - 5p

opened in 1998. owners: becky and jim buford
all major credit cards accepted
make-up specialist on saturdays

fremont >

as i look around my house, i know i have a problem. it's called beauty product addiction. there are easily four-dozen perfume bottles lined up on the shelves, even though i rarely wear perfume (pretty bottles!). in the shower there are a baker's dozen of body washes from gingerbread to fig. and don't get me started on skincare products. obviously, i need help. but before i begin my detox, i must visit *essenza* at least one more time. even though it's the seattle mecca for beauty products, i swear i'm going just to buy a new nightgown from their sleepwear line. really.

covet:
serge lutens perfumes
red flower bodycare products
tocca perfumes
trilogy skincare
duchess marden skincare products
sophie gardner jewelry
essenza sleepwear
l'oiseau bateau bedding

fancy pants

custom designs and handmade goods by local artists

1914 2nd avenue. between virginia and stewart
206.956.2945 www.fancyjewels.com / www.pantsunderpants.com
tue - sat 11a - 6p sun noon - 5p

opened in 2002. owner: sally brock
mc. visa
online shopping. gift registries. custom orders / design

belltown >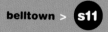

first there was a store called *fancy*. and then followed a store named *pants*. after awhile it seemed like a good idea to meld the two stores together, applause for *fancy pants*. like cold milk and captain crunch, or tomato soup and grilled cheese—these two stores belong together. the mix of sally's funky-chic urban jewelry, other local artisan-crafted goodies and then, pants (many of the under-variety) and a smattering of cute, sweet clothing—is just too good to miss. this is the best match made since cake and frosting.

fleurish

glorious flowers and arrangements
1308 east union street. between 13th and 14th
206.322.1602 www.fleurish.com
by appointment only

opened in 1997. owner: nisha kelen
all major credit cards accepted
custom orders / design. tailored events. deliveries

capitol hill > **s12**

for many years now, i have been admiring the floral genius of nisha. whenever i entered a restaurant or store and noticed a stunning floral arrangement, the creator of the piece would always be nisha. i knew i had to meet this person who was the producer of such magic, and so i went to her little outpost of botanical wonder, *fleurish*. i visited during the valentine's day rush and the place was abundant with blooms from sweet tulips to lilting, graceful orchids—it was like being in the garden of eden.

covet:
some of nisha's favorite flowers:
  white amaryllis
  queen of the night tulip
loosely wrapped bouquets
arrangements in all shapes & sizes
potted orchids & bulbs
lovely collection of vessels
neisha's sweet dog, violet

flit

tiny and sweet women's boutique
3526 fremont place north, unit d (enter on 36th)
between fremont avenue and fremont place north
206.547.2177 flitboutique.blogspot.com
wed - sat noon - 6p sun noon - 5p

opened in 2006. owner: pesha nguyen
all major credit cards accepted
online shopping. custom orders

fremont > **s13**

flit is a funny word. it's one of those words that you've got stored in your brain's memory bank, but you rarely have the need to use it. it's kind of like flibbertigibbet or whoopsy daisy. so i'm so glad that pesha found good use for this catchy word. she's tagged her teensy boutique *flit*, and it fits. the clothing is feminine, yet a bit urban—sweet, but with an edge so it doesn't fall into frilly. this is the type of clothing i like to wear on an daily basis. so i guess that makes me a flitter.

covet:
triple five soul
voom
odyn
manoush
tano handbags
super lucky cat
mk2k
pesha's pretty jewelry

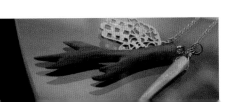

frock shop

feminine lovelies

6500 phinney avenue north. corner of 65th
206.297.1638 www.shopfrockshop.com
mon - sat 11a - 7p sun 11a - 4p

opened in 2005. owner: suzy fairchild
mc. visa
online shoping. gift registries. custom orders/design

phinney ridge > **s14**

i still regret the dress that i wore to my prom. it wasn't really a dress, but a white linen dirndl skirt and a matching blouse with lace sleeves. my father must have been beyond thrilled, because i looked like a prissy nun—only my big hair saved me from the miss prim-prom award 1982. if only *frock shop* had been open back then. their luscious velvet polka-dot dress with fuschia tulle should have been my prom dress, and then i could have danced like the hot latino girl in grease (instead of like olivia newton-john, in my get-up). get your pretty on at at *frock shop*.

covet:
suzy fairchild hats & bags
retropolitan marilyn monroe earrings
sofada polka-dot dress
vintage wrap & gift cards
kimmi clothing
koko bags
katherine harestad pretty undies
diane kappa pillows

george

unique gifts and local art
5633 airport way south. corner of lucille
206.763.8100 www.georgeintown.com
mon - sat 10a - 4p

opened in 2004. owners: holly krejci and kathy nyland
cash. check

georgetown >

for years i was obsessed with the name fred. i don't know why exactly, but fred just cracked me up. just lately though, the name george has been catching up with fred. hmmm, why is this? curious george? nah. george bush? please. it must be *george*, the store in seattle. i love any reason to cruise into georgetown. there's a little tribe of pioneering businesses down here—*all city coffee*, *jules maes saloon*, *georgetown records*, *helle skincare* to name a few. and *george* is their general store. okay, there's no food here—but there's candy! and cool gifts and art and...

covet:
georgetown:not just for hookers anymore t's
mike bristow assemblage
red horseshoe notebooks
shorthand press t's & cards
little diva cigarbox purses
donna sturgess enamel necklaces
sin city pendants
old-fashioned candy!!!

georgia blu

an enchanting children's boutique

4707 california avenue sw. at the alaska junction
206.935.4499 www.georgiablu.com
mon - sat 10a - 6p sun 11a - 5p

opened in 2006. owner: krista means
mc. visa
gift baskets. trunk shows

west seattle > **s16**

my entire life i have been besotted by cotton candy, not only because it was fun as heck to eat, but it was soooo beautiful. when i walked into *georgia blu*, i felt like i had walked into a little fifedom where there were marshmallow clouds and blue cotton candy mountains. this is a magical place and the kids' clothing is dreamy—modern pieces that have a whimsical edge and are comfy and cool. this is the type of clothing that kids love, so you'll have to pry it off their little bodies for a weekly cleaning!

covet:
clothing:
  neige
  tea
  luna luna / hubcap
  splendid littles t's
naturino shoes
powell craft nighties
little giraffe blankets

121

hitchcock

a jewelbox of wonderfulness

1123 34th avenue. between spring and union
206.838.7173 www.shophitchcock.com
wed - sun 10a - 6p (11a - 7p in the summer)

opened in 2006. owner: erica sheehan
mc. visa
online shopping. custom orders/design

madrona >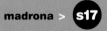

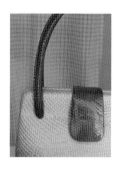

there's a line of bags carried at *hitchcock* that's called not rational. this should be my personal tagline for the impulses i have when entering here. i just want to throw all fiscal caution to the wind, and buy buy buy. erica has created a romantic, nooky den of gorgeous jewelry and accessories in madrona, and i'm telling you, ladies—whether you live on the eastside or the westside, find the time to stop by, as nobody else in town has the same fine eye and whimsical style of baubles, bangles and bags that erica has here.

covet:
subversive jewelry
regina chang jewelry
rings eclectic by melanie lynn
perfido design bangles
my mothers' buttons jewelry
not rational bags
vintage bags & jewelry
three custom color cosmetics

impulse

apparel for the discriminating and fashion-forward female

3516 fremont place north (enter on 36th)
between fremont avenue and fremont place north
206.545.4854 www.impulseseattle.com
mon - sat 11a - 7p sun 11a - 5p

opened in 2003. owner: jill wenger
all major credit cards accepted
online shopping

fremont > **s18**

a couple of years back, i was in austin working with my pal marianne. one day i put on a dress that i knew would ring miss m's bell. she loved it so much, she got right on the phone to jill at *impulse* to order one. two years later, marianne reports to me that even though she lives, works and shops in austin—she shops at *impulse* more than anywhere else. why, you ask? because jill gets it. she not only understands her customers, but she understands that women want the new modern classics. clothing that's urban and sharp, yet has a feminine touch.

covet:
tsumori chisato
acne jeans
anglomania by vivienne westwood
mayle
a.p.c.
saya hibano jewelry
y's by yohji yamamoto accessories
opening ceremony footwear

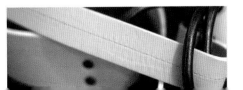

juniper

simple and chic women's clothing and home décor

3314 east spring street. corner of 34th
206.838.7496 www.juniperinmadrona.com
wed - sun 10a - 6p or by appointment

opened in 2007. owner: lisa clinton
all major credit cards accepted

madrona > **s19**

lately, terms like sustainable, organic and green have become more commonplace in our american vernacular. from little kids to big adults, folks are beginning to understand that we need to protect our planet and its ever more limited natural resources. lisa is contributing to this movement at *juniper*, which is first and foremost, a lovely boutique. lisa sources lines which are ecologically sound, and let me tell you, you feel good wearing them. i bought a gray cotton zoe tee dress here, and i suspect it will be worn until someday somebody will need to recycle me.

covet:
zoe tees
loomstate jeans
anna cohen clothing
loyale clothing
stewart + brown clothing
virginia johnson
dominique picquier bags
matta home

kimberly baker jewelry

enchanting jewelry with a twist

617 north 36th street. between fremont avenue and fremont place north
206.545.1145 www.kimberlybaker.com
wed - sat noon - 6p sun noon - 5p

opened in 2006. owner: kimberly baker
mc. visa
online shopping. custom orders

fremont >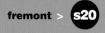

here's my dream: i'm walking down a heavily wooded path toward a river. i'm not looking for anything in particular, yet i seem to be on a search. suddenly there's a wolf, but in the dream it's gold and it becomes a ring and slips onto my finger. then swooping overhead comes a phoenix with dangling earrings. at the river, a unicorn stands with its horn glistening. is this a dream or is it *kimberly baker jewelry*? who cares? as i'll happily live in the dream if i get to sport kimberly's amazing creations.

covet:
wolfette ring
fat jacks necklace
unicorn horn earrings & necklace
phoenix rising earrings
audrey necklace
ziggy earrings
carmen necklace
juanita earrings

kobo

japanese and northwest fine crafts

at higo: 602-608 south jackson street. between 6th and maynard. 206.381.3000
capitol hill: 814 east roy street. corner of broadway. 206.726.0704
www.koboseattle.com
higo: mon - sat 11a - 6p capitol hill: tue - fri noon - 7p sat 11a - 7p sun noon - 6p

opened in 1995. owners: binko chiong-bisbee and john bisbee
all major credit cards accepted
online shopping. special gift wrapping. gallery shows

international district / capitol hill > s21

not long ago the streets around *kobo at higo* in the international district were a bustling area known as japantown, or, *nihonmachi*. it was a vibrant community until the '40s when many of the areas residents were interred in camps during the panic of the war. today the streets are bustling again, and the *higo* store, which is a landmark in the area, is vibrant again with *kobo* moving into its space. the store now features *kobo's* renowned japanese crafts and designs but is also a museum honoring *higo* and the moving stories of the area's past.

covet:
laura yeats big ash bowl
hakusan rock handle mugs
jin bao shu personalized seals
ninsho paintings on wood blocks
agelio batle graphite objects
sugahara sake glass
zouri straw sandals
baobab pods

lambs ear

shoes and accessories by upcoming designers

3516 fremont place north (enter on 36th)
between fremont avenue and fremont place north
206.632.2626 www.lambsearshoes.com
mon - fri 11a - 6p sat 11a - 7p sun noon - 5p

opened in 2007. owner: angie sorensen
all major credit cards accepted
online shopping

fremont >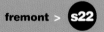

as you already know, i'm a big fan of *impulse*. not only because the clothes are so frickin' perfect, but also because i love the subterranean location. still, it always felt like there was a hole to fill next door. hmmm, what would be perfect? no doubt—shoes, beautiful shoes. angie heeded the call with *lambs ear*. the space is modern with a look all its own, and the shoes and accessories are the freshest around. if you've heard about a high-style, big-city shoe and are searching for it, this is the place you'll no doubt find it.

covet:
shoes:
  loeffler randall
  marcello toshi
  chie mihara
  corso como
anna corinna bags
kimberly baker jewelry
poupette jewelry

la rousse

fashion-forward women's clothing

430 virginia street. between 4th and 5th
206.448.1515 www.la-rousse.com
mon - sat 11a - 7p sun noon - 5p

opened in 2005. owner: amanda rosenthal
all major credit cards accepted
custom orders/design

belltown >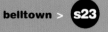

sometime in the last couple of years, i began to be obsessed with wearing comfortable clothes. i'm not talking velour sweats with type plastered on my der-riere, but stylish and modern clothing that i can slip on easily and layer to my heart's content. this was exactly the clothing that i found at *la rousse*. amanda mixes together beloved easy pieces and then throws in some more structured designs, to take you from day to night and in between. heavy, deep sigh of fashion contentment.

covet:
rodebjer
karen walker
mona & holly
webster
christopher deane
anna sui
del forte denim
parkvogel

lavender heart

european-style botanicals, gifts and home accessories
2812 east madison. between mlk, jr boulevard and 29th
206.568.4441
tue - sat 10:30a - 6p sun 11a - 4p

opened in 1998. owner: holly henderson
mc. visa

madison valley >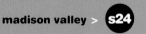

around the world there are a small number of people who have spectacular olfactory abilities. many of these people work in the perfume industry, as they can define the purity of smell notes with just a whiff. holly at *lavender heart* could be one of these people. though she's smelled thousands of scents, she can define what is the purest lavender or the cleanest lemon. and these are the products you will find here mixed in with extraordinary botanicals that make you feel like you're exploring in a garden of goodness.

covet:
mistral pamplemousse cassis rouge anything
tade glassware & soaps
shira leah puffball bag
maletti balsamico di modena
faux paper hydrangea
color washed bamboo
wreathes, topiaries, mounds &
  european style hedges

les amis

urban romantic women's clothing and accessories

3420 evanston avenue north. between 34th and 35th
206.632.2877 www.lesamis-inc.com
mon - wed 11a - 6p thu - sat 11a - 7p sun 11a - 5p

opened in 1995. owners: becky and jim buford
mc. visa

fremont >

les amis tortures me. during production on my books, i try to keep my actual buying to a minimum because if i didn't, i would be bankrupt many times over. so when i enter *les amis*, i hold up the hope that there won't be a thing that i fancy. please, that's never going to happen—becky might as well just take over my wardrobe. each piece is more beautiful than the next here, and yet it's extremely wearable beauty. take a chic piece by rozae nichols and then mix it with a butter soft t-shirt and you get the idea.

covet:
gary graham
rozae nichols
dosa
krista larsen
erica tanov
mike + chris
inhabit
giorgio brato bags

139

maison luxe

a fresh mix of modern and classic furnishings and life accessories

1123 first avenue. corner of seneca
206.405.2828 www.maisonluxe.net
tue - sat 10a - 6p sun noon - 5p

opened in 2006. owner: kelie grosso
all major credit cards accepted
custom orders/design. interior design consultation

north pioneer square > **s26**

my husband and i have an ongoing rift about what modern design is. my stubborn opinion is that many things that are contemporary have influences from the past, but are reimagined. he feels modern means wholly new, fantastically space-age design. whoever is right (no doubt, me) i know we could both agree on *maison luxe*. kelie has created a world here that's both modern and classic, where supple white leather moroccan poufs intermingle with slighty rococco, super-sexy sofas. this is the type of mix i could happily live with.

covet:
cisco brothers furniture (all custom-order)
urban hardwoods
wonderful vintage pieces
oly studio chairs
leather moroccan poufs
arteriors lamps
global view mirrors
mor cosmetics sugar crystal marshmallow scrub

merge

contemporary women's apparel

5000 20th avenue nw. corner of ballard
206.782.5335 www.mergeboutique.com
mon - wed 11a - 6p thu - fri 11a - 7p sat 11a - 6p sun noon - 5p

opened in 2006. owner: patricia wolfkill
all major credit cards accepted
online shopping

ballard >

from the moment i began talking to patricia, it was like the saying: we got on like a house on fire. here's a woman who has a sharp, smart take on fashion—and it shows at *merge*. she's featuring lines here that are beautifully made and conceived—you'll be hard-pressed to find these pieces anywhere else in town. i was so besotted with every piece by ports 1961, that i kept on having to go back by the rack just just so i could touch the fabric and gaze at them longingly and pray to the clothing gods that someday they would hang in my closet.

covet:
ports 1961
elijah
tony cohen
olga kapustina
nicholas k
jarbo
lamade
american vintage

mimi rose

delightful children's clothing, toys, books and gifts

6001 phinney avenue. corner of 60th
206.361.1834
tue - sat 10a - 6p or by appointment

opened in 2005. owner: margaret rose
all major credit cards accepted
gift registries

phinney ridge > **s28**

when my daughter lola was born, i dressed her in a lot of groovy, unisex clothing. around the time she could begin to talk, she was able to insist on wearing nothing but tutus and dresses. i wish i had known about *mimi rose* at this point, because it would have fulfilled both of our wishes. the majority of the clothes here are designed by margaret and are sweetly old-fashioned with a modern twist and a touch of whimsy for good measure. the little boutique that showcases these clothes and the plethora of great toys and gifts is truly a candyland.

covet:
children's clothing & accessories:
  mimi rose
  bow-wow club
empress arts cable-knit sweater & hats
eeboo toys
schylling retro toys
selecta push toys
käthe kruse dolls

moxie papergoods & gifts

modern card shop and more

3916 california avenue sw. between bradford and andover
206.932.2800 www.moxiepapergoods.com
tue - fri 10a - 7p sat 10a - 5p

opened in 2006. owners: jodie marr and kimberly lim
mc. visa
gift wrapping. custom stationery and invitations

west seattle >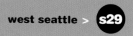

over the years, i have developed a gift box. this is where i keep my "need-on-the-fly-don't-have-time-to-shop" presents. this box empties quickly, so i'm always on the lookout for a great gift store to help me restock. *moxie papergoods & gifts* fits the bill perfectly. i'll take some candles, some beautiful letterpressed notecards, a couple of cute baby items, a luscious-smelling lotion or two and *voila!* i'm done. wait, i must get some cool paper to wrap them all in. and then hold on, shouldn't i be gifting myself a little something also?

covet:
moxie home gift packs
snow & graham candles & cards
bloodshot press cards
urban smalls baby hats
modern alchemy perfume faux pocket watches
xonex pencils
dani plum flower lotion
petal tarocco candles

nancy

whimsical handcrafted products and decorations

1930 2nd avenue. between virginia and stewart
206.441.7131 www.nancynancynancy.com
tue - sat 11a - 4p

opened in 2006. owners: kate greiner and aaron murray
all major credit cards accepted
classes. custom invitations and decorations

belltown > s30

the newest member of the *fancypantsschmancy* strip along second avenue is *nancy*. from the moment i peeked in the window, i knew i would looove what i found inside. i was immediately besotted with the little ceramic animal figurines that kate's husband aaron makes—it's like aaron's wild kingdom, and he makes groovy shadow boxes for all the little guys to live in. i wanted to shrink myself and live with the owl and bunny families in one. i'll have to find some shrinking juice for the next time i visit.

covet:
almond joyce cards & decorations
aaron murray animal figurines & shadow boxes
alice tippit small portraits
la familia green cards
tory franklin cards
elizabeth roberts beehives
decorative fossils
raindrop garlands

okok

where design and art collide in a spectacular way

5107 ballard avenue nw. corner of dock
206.789.6242 www.weareokok.com
tue - sat noon - 6p sun 11a - 5p

opened in 2004. owners: charlie and amanda kitchings
all major credit cards accepted
online shopping. custom orders / design. gallery

ballard > s31

to my new friends at *okok*. thank you for naming your store after me. i know that the reason you did this is because you knew that i would be cuckoo for your fresh and cool mix of design and art, and blurring all the lines in between. thank you for stocking jason miller's work because i really want to own all of it. but i want to not thank you for that stunning salvaged cedar table in the middle of your store. the one that i deeply desire to own, but don't have a 15' foot dining room to accomodate it. oh well. thanks, though, for everything else here that's swell.

covet:
jason miller porcelain hostess cupcakes
marcel dzama canister set
urbana design serving tray
third drawer down tea towels & lapkins
monacca cedar kaku laptop bag
piet houtenbos grenade oil lamp
the 15' salvaged cedar table
kinfolk pillows

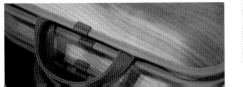

ornamo

moving design forward

301 occidental avenue south. corner of main
206.859.6492 www.ornamo.com
tue - sat 11a - 6p or by appointment

opened in 2006. owner: brian balmert
mc. visa
custom orders / design

pioneer square > **s32**

there are tiny, magic moments in this life where you meet a person and you immediately fall into deep connect mode. the day i walked into *ornamo* and met brian was one of those moments. it wasn't just brian i felt this synergy with, but also *ornamo*—a place that i wouldn't dare define with just any run-of-the-mill word. *ornamo* is where you come if you care about great design. brian picks the lines that he sells with thoughtful precision, and your home will absolutely benefit from his wickedly good eye.

covet:
timorous beasties wallpaper
bombast furniture
urban hardwoods
nani marquina rugs
artelano furniture
aq hayon collection
gruppo di installazione soft goods
established + sons furniture

oslo's

stylish, yet un-fussy men's attire
1519 queen anne avenue. between galer and garfield
206.282.OSLO www.oslosamensstore.com
mon - wed, fri 10a - 7p thu 10a - 9p sat 10a - 6p sun 11a - 5p

opened in 2005. owner: john a. mcdowell, jr.
all major credit cards accepted
grooming services by chad (wed - sun)

queen anne > **s33**

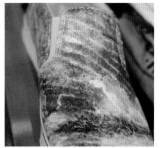

most women i know, after a cocktail or two during a girls' night out, will at some point start griping about their man. a favorite rant is about men's inability to multitask. we congratulate ourselves on our dominance in this area—but ladies, beware. *oslo's* features a whole new level of male multitasking… shopping for clothes and getting a shave and haircut simultaneously. eeek, what will we have to bitch about when our male arrives nattily dressed in styling threads and sporting the cleanest shave (thx to chad) he's had since before he grew hair on his chin?

covet:
james perse everything
theory clothing
mason's khakis & shirts
kinetics t's & sweats
morgan grays handsome style bags
napapijri clothing
the art of shaving products
a wickedly good shave by chad

peter miller

top-drawer architectural and design bookstore and more

1930 first avenue. between virginia and stewart
206.441.4114 www.petermiller.com
mon - sat 10a - 6p

opened in 1980. owner: peter miller
all major credit cards accepted
online shopping

belltown >

i'm a graphic designer and am obsessed with books about, you guessed it, design. so where do i go to get my design book fix? the internet? please... i need to leaf through the book, touch the paper, smell the ink. unless amazon is going to develop touch 'n' sniff technology, i'm going to need to get off my tushy and head to *peter miller*. every creative i know on the west coast shops at this mecca. been trying to get an interview with that smokin' art director at the hot ad agency in town? don't bother calling him at his office, as you'll find him in the stacks here.

covet:
villas / saunas in finland (peter's favorite book)
shallow water dictionary
domus vol. 1- 6
handbook for the graphic arts
ultimate london design
speak italian: the fine art of the gesture
3 x 10 roaster
iittala glasses

polite society

style haven for both sexes

1924 first avenue. between stewart and virginia
206.441.4796 www.shoppolitesociety.com
mon - sat 11a - 7p sun 11a - 5p

opened in 2006. owner: eric akines
all major credit cards accepted
online shopping. gift registries. custom orders / design

belltown > **s35**

when i enter a clothing store, i will go down the racks and when i find a piece that captures my attention, either by touch or by sight, i pull it out and look at the label. it's not that i'm a brand snob, i'm just intrigued to know if i can guess the designer. at *polite society*, the clothes are stunning and the labels are all ones that are entirely new to me—this is thrilling. eric is the hunter and gatherer extraordinaire. he searches the world for the most unique fashions, and what he finds to bring back to his lush emporium will literally take your breath away.

covet:
aoi
afshin feiz
baum und pferdgarten
bell
malene birger
wintle
costume national
les hommes

159

private screening

vintage clothing and furnishings
3504 fremont place north. between fremont avenue and 36th
206.548.0751
mon - sat 11a - 6p sun 11a - 5p

opened in 1991. owners: gary and michele mortenson
mc. visa

fremont > 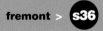 **s36**

as i was walking by *private screening*, i caught a glimpse of the perfect horizontal-stripe t-shirt. i needed no more invitation than this to enter and buy. the vintagesque french fishmerman's shirt with the red and white stripes was a no-brainer; it had to be mine. but this was just the tip of the iceberg. the store has mainly vintage finds, but mixed in are some new pieces with a retro vibe. soon, i had more than just the t-shirt in purchase position. a small stack of great finds was more like it.

covet:
particularly primo vintage:
  suits, ladies' dresses & shoes
  jewels & scarves
  undergarments
  chinoiserie dresses
robert p. miller vintagesque striped t's
zodiac symbol necklaces
viewmaster slides

red ticking

vintage french fabrics and home interiors
2802 east madison. corner of 28th avenue south
206.250.8853 www.redticking.com
mon - tue interior design appointments only
wed - fri 11a - 6p sat 11a - 5:30p

opened in 2003. owner: pamela robinson
mc. visa
interior design services. custom orders / design

madison valley > s37

i think it's apropos to have been talking about french striped fisherman's t-shirts in the last blurb, and then move straight on to *red ticking* which is the go-to place in seattle for vintage french fabrics. i should have worn my new shirt here, and then i could have sat on one of pam's amazingly comfortable couches upholstered in the aforementioned ticking, and i would have looked like a human checkerboard. there are so many beautiful things here, it's hard to know where to look first. so i suggest kicking back on the couch and having pam show you what's wonderful in her world.

covet:
fabrics:
  vintage french ticking & batiks
  european grainbags
custom upholstery & lampshades
mercury glass lighting
rani arabella cashmere throws
cherry dinnerware
barefoot contessa everything

riveted

a modern jeans store

1113 1st avenue. between spring and seneca
206.624.JEAN (8853) www.rivetedjeans.com
mon - sat 10a - 6p sun 11a - 5p

opened in 2005. owners: lex petras and allison cornia
all major credit cards accepted
online shopping. custom orders. alterations

almost pioneer square > **s38**

back in the day when i was racing around like made on my schwinn bike with a banana seat, levi's were the only jeans that i would wear. when i moved to nyc for college, the jeans stayed behind and denim didn't touch my body again until i moved to l.a., as you're not allowed to enter the city without a healthy denim collection. i could have used *riveted* back then. they sell denim not so much because their jeans are the "it" jeans of the season, but because they are well-made denim that's going to make the wearer, whatever body type, feel superfine.

covet:
jeans:
  april 7
  cheap monday
  robins
  stronghold
  iron army
  monotype
  pine iv

rue

women's clothing that's a little uptown and a bit downtown

611 stewart street. between 6th and 7th
206.264.0788 www.rueseattle.com
tue - sat 10a - 7p sun noon - 6p mon by appointment

opened in 2007. owner: michelle kim
all major credit cards accepted
online shopping. custom orders / design

downtown > **s39**

when i first moved back to the northwest after being in nyc and la for years, i missed the fashion shows i would see daily on the streets in those über-cities. but as the last century came to a close, i began to notice the presence of some very fashion-forward gals here. they had taken big-city style and meshed it into something distinctively northwest, yet really fresh. i'm pretty sure that these ladies are now shopping at *rue*, because this is the type of clothing that michelle specializes in. smart and chic, and yet affordable enough so there's no guilt induced by a spree.

covet:
amanda uprichard
lewis cho
yanak
karen zambos
yumi kim
corey lynn clater
bobi
vintage pieces upstairs

167

schmancy

toys that look like art, art that looks like toys
1932 2nd avenue. between virginia and stewart
206.728.8008 www.schmancytoys.com
tue - sat 11a - 6p sun noon - 5p (hours vary seasonally)

opened in 2004. owner: kristen rask
all major credit cards accepted
online shopping

belltown >

schmancy is not spelled schmanzy. for all those that caught my darn typo in the last edition, thank you for your emails and letters. maybe i could convince the other businesses on the street to change their names to nanzy and fanzy pants. nah. *schmancy* is swell as is, and it's the place i want to go to when i need something to make me smile. looking for a cigarette plushy? or a super-size, stuffed gold tooth? they're here and are guaranteed to elicit a guffaw or two. and if you are a plushy fan (like me), you'll want to check out kristen's plushblog at plushyou.blogspot.com.

covet:
jim woodring mr. bumper
tokidoki moofia
sewdorky school of dentistry pimp tooth
heidi kenney donut key chains
lauda shikito salvatorem bshit
bisbee stitches animals
tad lauritzen wright fuzz cigarettes
plush you by kristen rask

169

space oddity

vintage furniture and doodads

5318 22nd avenue nw. corner of ballard
206.331.8054 www.spaceoddityballard.com
tue - fri 2 - 6p sat 1 - 6p sun noon - 4p

opened in 2003. owner: todd werny
mc. visa
sourcing

ballard >

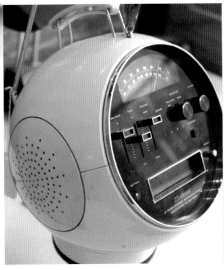

i like to go out thrifting or doing the garage sale loop sometimes if in the right state of mind. if lucky, i score and find a great piece, but most often i don't find much more than a collection of burl ives christmas albums and lots of plastic crapola. this is why going to *space oddity* is more appealing to me. here is where i can find the vintage furniture and knicknacks that i desire. and the best thing is that cool todd hasn't priced his great finds into the stratosphere, so i can actually own the stuff i want. brilliant.

covet:
'50s wood library drawer set
'50s gym lockers
groovy aluminum tray holder on wheels
weltron eight-track stereo
vintage library card file cabinet & credenza
horsehead chessboard table
dansk flamestone pottery

swee swee paperie & studio

contemporary paper goods and wrapping studio
4218 sw alaska. corner of california (at the alaska junction)
206.937.7933 www.sweesweepaperie.com
tue - fri 11a - 6p sat 11a - 5p

opened in 2006. owner: ann conway
mc. visa
gift wrapping. corporate gifting. custom invitations

west seattle > **s42**

i know this is a bit pathetic, but i am the world's worst present wrapper. to begin with, i wait until the last moment (i.e. ten minutes before leaving for a birthday party), and then i just messily wrap some colored tissue paper around the gift and throw it into a gift bag. *voila!* pathetic. i obviously need help, and *swee swee* is has been put on this earth to give it to me and to those of you who are also giftwrapping-challenged. bring your gifts here, and even better, buy them here—ann and gang will gorgeously wrap them in the coolest papers around.

covet:
heidi gift wrap
whimsy press wrapping paper
herman yu design cards
good on paper cards
bald guy cards
midori press papers & ribbons
russell + hazel office products
xonex office products

tableau

gifts and embellishments for the home

2220 nw market street. between ballard and 22nd
206.782.5846 www.tableaugifts.com
mon - fri 10:30a - 6p sat 10a - 5:30p sun noon - 5p

opened in 1999. owner: karen olsen
all major credit cards accepted

ballard >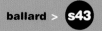

tableau got me in trouble last christmas. i was shopping in ballard with my mother and my daughter, and i took them to *tableau* for the first time. five minutes into the shopping experience, lola was already laden down with multiple sparkling bird ornaments and my mother was juggling numerous finds. both chastised me for not bringing them to *tableau* before. me bad mother / daughter / shopping guide. after begging forgiveness, i was able to concentrate on adding to the haul. when it comes to home décor and gift giving, karen really covers all the bases.

covet:
astier de villate dishware
penkridge ceramics horse chestnut
red egg furniture
working class studio pillows
karl blossfeldt prints
bird stools
sukie sketchbook
gorgeous jewelry

tricoter

beloved knitting institution
3121 east madison street. corner of lake washington boulevard
206.328.6505 www.tricoter.com
mon - wed 10a - 5:30p thu 10a - 7p fri - sat 10a - 5p

opened in 1984. owners: lindy phelps and beryl hiatt
all major credit cards accepted
classes. finishing services. custom pattern-making. custom orders / design
—

madison valley > **s44**

in the first edition of this guide i noted that i intended to take up knitting because i was motivated and inspired by *tricoter's* incredible universe of all things knitting related. now it's three years later, and i... still do not knit. but, it's not for lack of desire. i obviously needed to revisit *tricoter* to get re-inspired, and so i did. there is the most extraordinary selection here of yarns. match that up with fantastic patterns and a veritable plethora of classes. note to self: stop the silly laziness, take up knitting now!

covet:
yarns:
  louisa harding
  s. charles
  filatura di crosa
  tanglewood fibers
  socks that rock
buttons, buttons, buttons!
any of the tricoter knitting books

tulip

fresh and lovely women's clothing
1201 first avenue. corner of seneca
206.223.1790 www.tulip-seattle.com / shoptulip.blogspot.com
mon - sat 10a - 6p sun noon - 5p

opened in 2002. owner: annie sparrow
all major credit cards accepted
online shopping

almost pioneer square > **s45**

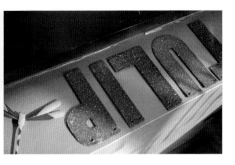

as i'm driving into seattle, my car magically, without me steering, veers toward first avenue. some of my favorite shopping in this city is on this stretch, and *tulip* is always right at the top of this list. i can count on the charming annie to always know what i, and other like-minded women, want to wear—her finger is never off the ever-changing pulse of fashion. she and her lovely gaggle of shop gals will make sure to find just the right something that will tickle your fancy without making your bank account feel empty.

covet:
dallin chase
mike & chris
alexander wang
jovovich-hawk
bing bang jewelry
trovata
dirty librarian jewelry
malin + goetz skincare

tune

hi-fi for humans

2121 first avenue, suite 101. between bell and leonora
206.283.8863 www.tunehifi.com
tue - sat 11a - 6p or by appointment

opened in 2004. owner: connon price
all major credit cards accepted
music / home theater system design and installation

belltown >  **s46**

i'm a stereophonic numbskull. over the years, i've picked up a stereo or two—but i couldn't tell you the maker or why i chose that particular model. secretly though, i yearn for a sharp-sounding system—one that fills the house with beautiful music. also i want a turntable to play my old adam ant albums. the place to go for this is *tune*. over the years, i had heard about connon through the grapevine, and finally visited his store. this place is not only for stereophiles, it's also for people like you and me who need someone to lead us down the correct path of good sound.

covet:
naim audio
slim devices squeezebox
wilson benesch turntable
beyerdynamic headphones
speakers:
  focal
  totem acoustics
  t+a elektroakustik

tuuli

finnish products featuring marimekko

1407 first avenue. between pike and union
206.223.1112 www.tuuliseattle.com
mon - wed, sat 10a - 6p thu - fri 10a - 8p sun 11:30a - 6p

opened in 2004. owner: ulla freeman
mc. visa
custom orders / design

pike place market > **s47**

as you've read many times in this book, i'm loopy about all things scandinavian, especially the design. this fascination began with marimekko. i grew up in the '70s with these designs, and my mother told me that back then, marimekko was radically different than anything anybody had seen before. i remember thinking that the big poppy prints and bright colors made me happy. today, you can get your marimekko fix at *tuuli*. they stock, if not everything, most everything in the line, from towels, to clothes to rainboots to plateware. it's a finnish dream.

covet:
marimekko:
  jokapoika striped shirts
  bags & coin purses
  rainboots & umbrellas
limbo helsinki dresses & tops
nanso raincoats
aarikka jewelry
housewares by finnish independent designers

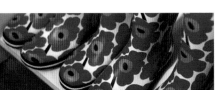

two owls

a sweet boutique for little ones
3308 east spring street. corner of 34th
206.624.2182 www.shoptwoowls.com
tue - sun 10a - 5p (hours vary)

opened in 2007. owner: mona anastas
all major credit cards accepted
online shopping

madrona >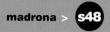

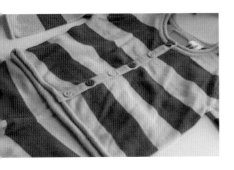

on the day i visited *juniper*, i happened to notice right next door a teensy little store. i walked in and it was love at first sight. all the qualities that we love in children, their purity of spirit, their funny little senses of humour—all this exists in the goods that *two owls* sells. from comfy clothes with zippy colors to toys that you would actually love to have strewn around the house, everything here is designed to make childhood, and for that matter, parenthood, as sunny and fun as a warm spring day at the park.

covet:
two owls organic cotton clothing
happygreenbee clothing
under the nile clothing
irie star clothing
barbara sansome toys
haba toys
kashmiri keepsake boxes
moonlight & roses fairy boards

urchin

modern home, accessories and gifts

1922 first avenue. between stewart and virginia
206.448.5800 www.urchinseattle.com
mon - sat 10a - 6p sun noon - 5p

opened in 2005. owner: karen cho
all major credit cards accepted
online shopping. gift registries. custom orders

belltown > **s49**

when i was visiting *urchin*, i was having a great time chatting with karen. in talking to her, i asked her what she thought was one of her best-selling items. i expected her to tell me that it was one of the beautifully utilitarian bags, but no. my next guess was the mud australia porcelain that was so perfectly crafted i imagined it must be top of the list. nope. it was the totally cool xenia taler ceramic tiles. tiles you say? and then it made sense. at a lifestyle design store like *urchin*, people are searching for what's fresh and new. and these tiles were all that and more.

covet:
mud australia porcelain
bahari teak bowls
michael aram tableware
polli australia stainless & aluminum jewelry
mandarina duck bags
mishi leather bags
dreamsacks silk throws
xenia taler ceramic tiles

velouria

boutique and gallery featuring local artisans

2205 nw market street. corner of 22nd avenue
206.788.0330 www.shopvelouria.com
mon - wed 11a - 6p thu - fri 11a - 8p sat 11a - 7p sun noon - 6p

opened in 2004. owner: tes de luna
mc. visa
online shopping. gift wish list. custom orders / design

ballard > 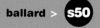 s50

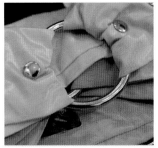

in the last couple of years, there's been an increasing focus on local and independent designers and artisans. it's really cool to know that in each city i visit, i can always look for a boutique that is going to feature the fruits of these labors, and *velouria* is just that in seattle. from sweet, lacy little slips to bird-inspired jewelry—there's talent aplenty on display here and tes is the ringleader. not only does she corral this all into one space, she is also a designer herself. be on the lookout for her zuzu pop line while exploring all the other goodies on display.

covet:
zuzu pop silkscreened t's
frocky jack morgan recycled layered dresses
liza rietz clothing
pare umbrellas
queen bee bags
my olivette jewelry
flora & fawn enameled birds
purldrop crocheted earrings

189

veritables

stylish home décor and accessories

object: 2816 east madison street. 206.726.8047
décor: 2806 east madiston street. 206.322.7782
www.veritablesdecor.com
mon - sat 10:30a - 6:30p sun noon - 5p

opened in 1993. owner: marie harris
all major credit cards accepted
online shopping. interior design services. custom orders / design

madison valley > **s51**

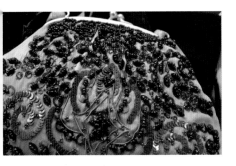

i like to talk about design. someone whom i always love to design talk with is marie at *veritables*. she's a veritable (another pun, sorry!) dictionary when it comes to interior and home design. she can rattle off the provenance of a table i covet in no time flat, and then share with me why that particular piece is special. you can feel these sensibilities in each of her filled-to-the-brim-with-goodness stores just steps away from each other. if you need something for your gift stash, head to *object*. if it's something for your home, then *décor*. or do like me, and visit both.

covet:
ankasa pillows
fun & funky cocktail rings
cashmere everything!
visual comfort lighting
horn tables
dransfield & ross root tables
white porcelain everything!
norwegian rabbit throw

watson kennedy

european-style home accessories and more more more

fine home: 1022 first avenue. corner of spring. 206.652.8350
fine living: 86 pine street. courtyard at the inn at the market. 206.443.6281
(see website for bellevue address) www.watsonkennedy.com
mon - sat 10a - 6p sun noon - 5p

opened in 1998. owner: ted kennedy watson
all major credit cards accepted
online shopping. custom orders

belltown / mr. ted's neighborhood / bellevue > s52

when i was chatting with kelie at *maison luxe*, we were trying to define the neighborhood that her store was in. was it west end? pioneer square? she thought for a moment, and then said it was mr. ted's neighborhood. so true. mr. ted is the proprietor of *watson kennedy* and the unofficial mayor in this territory. he knows everyone, but everyone knows his stores. for years, *watson kennedy* has been destination shopping because ted is the master of all things beautiful: his stores are emporiums of everything you need and even more things that you want.

covet:
la compagnie de provence products & candles
jeanine payer hand-inscribed jewelry
vintage limoge & spode tableware
le jacquard francais dish towels
mariage freres marco polo rouge
the proust questionnaire
letterpress cards galore!
princess pickled crunchy carrots

notes

etc.

the eat.shop guides were created by kaie wellman and are published by cabazon books
for more information about the series: www.eatshopguides.com

eat.shop seattle was written, researched and photographed by kaie wellman

copy editing: lynn king   fact checking: pat de garmo
map design and production: play with numbers - jim anderson, erin cheek and kieran lynn

kaie thx: each and every business in this book. the i-5 corridor. caffeine. and comfortable beds.

cabazon books: eat.shop seattle 3rd edition
ISBN-13 978-0-9766534-9-3

the eat.shop guides are distributed by independent publishers group: www.ipgbook.com

PRINTED IN SINGAPORE